Mundane to Magical

Creating Moments of Awareness in Everyday Life

TANYA HANSON

ISBN, print ed: 978-1-7333649-1-1
ISBN, ebook ed: 978-1-7333649-2-8

Library of Congress Catalog Number: 2019910622
Back Cover photo by Elly Mailhot
Cover by Stephanie Hannus

First Printing September 2019
Printed in the United States of America
Published by Ingramspark

To order visit www.tanyahanson.co

Morgan Marie and Blake Mae
You are Light. Shine Bright.

Acknowledgements

With much love and appreciation to my parents, Norm and Eileen, for your support, encouragement, friendship and love.

To Sharon Malecek and Gary Melin for loving my parents, I am grateful for your support and friendship.

Gabby and Ariel, you have been my greatest teachers. You make me proud to be your mother. Thanks for choosing me.

Jen, Christena, Sarah and Jodi, the greatest sister cousins ever, thank you for your laughter, love and support. Love yous.

To Jeannie Ouellette, with great appreciation for your kindness, gentle leading, and strong teaching, I am able to put these words into the world for others to read.

Michele Grace and Jen Yost as coaches and friends, you are amazing. Heartfelt gratitude sent your way.

To Becky Hughes, years ago you said, "You're going to write a book one day", I guess this is it. Thank you for your timely friendship, walks and talks.

Mary Beth Nehl, dearest teacher, my heart is full with immense love and gratitude for all you have shared with me. Thank you for opening the door and welcoming me in.

Fellow students from the Yoga Loft, I appreciate your openness to love, learn and share. Thank you for helping make The Loft, always feel like home. Namaste.

Thank you to the Hanson and Blankenhagen Families for your love and support.

To the Malecek and Jacob Families, your example of living and loving as family continues to inspire me.

To Florence Jacobs and Florence Malecek, I am lucky to call you Oma and Grandma. You have taught me what it looks like to be strong women. I love you.

Chuck, Thank you for your constant love and support of me and all my dreams.

Contents

Introduction

❧

—Two roads diverged in a wood, and I—
I took the one less traveled by,
And that has made all the difference.

—ROBERT FROST, "THE ROAD NOT TAKEN"

I first read this line of poetry in a book in my father's office. On its cover was a picture of trees darkened by shadows, a golden glow from the sun just beyond the horizon peeking through the branches. I cannot recall what age I was, or why out of the dozens of books on my father's shelves I remember this one.

I have taken this poem to heart. Not always consciously and purposefully, but I have never let myself be stopped from choosing the less expected path. I chose paths that were less traveled, not for the sake of adventure or courage, but because my heart led me there, as did the people on the journey who met me with questions and invitations along the way. An English teacher who asked me to consider taking a part in the school play. The speech coach who asked if I might like to explore how the speech team might give me new ways to express myself. What looked a bit like bravery was also my desire to find a place to fit in.

Sometimes the desire to *not* have to do something also led to the path less traveled. I could not fathom sewing one more thing in home economics class—or, rather, I was trying to keep myself from the frustration of ripping out yet another badly sewn seam.

And so I dropped home ec and became the only girl in the agriculture classes.

The desire for change was also an incentive to take the path others found daring. I left a stable job with good benefits to go back to school and open my own business. Recently, we moved three hours away from a town we'd lived in for more than twenty years so I could support my husband in following his dream. And now I am writing this book of personal stories, many of which I have never told before.

My stories are just bits and pieces of my path, my life. Our experiences shape our beliefs, how we react, or respond, how our points of view emerge. Life is an unfolding of new encounters and events. It is not a level, paved walking path clear of all debris. There are inclines, valleys, twists and hairpin turns, muddy sink holes and towering vistas.

We all have our own path. We get to make choices when the road diverges. No matter which path you take, embrace it and make it your own, because either way, it becomes your path.

Make Your Own Fun

❧

"A creative life is an amplified life. It's a bigger life, a happier life, an expanded life, and a hell of a lot more interesting life."

—Elizabeth Gilbert

I remember a family reunion when I was a child. Relatives from different states came together for a potluck picnic at a park with a trickling creek that wound through the woods, a twisting slide and swings, and a picnic shelter overlooking a tree-covered bluff. Adults talked and laughed. I was shy and hung close to Oma. Other children played, laughed, and ran around the playground, but not knowing them I was nervous to approach them to see if I could join in. Finally, Oma ordered me to go play. "Make your own fun," she said. It was the first time I remember hearing that phrase. It certainly was not the last.

It was and still is a family motto. Oma and parents alike spouted it to me and my cousins whenever we were at Oma's farm or any other family gathering. Bored kids: Find something to do and go make your own fun. Crying kids: Stop crying and go make your own fun. Crabby kids: Stop pouting and, you guessed it, go make your own fun!

Make our own fun we did. Sometimes we put on plays, with an older cousin directing, using toys as props, blankets as costumes. We would announce to the adults that we had a special show planned for them and after the performance we always received a rousing round of applause and a firm declaration that no encore was needed.

We played house in the same grove of trees my aunts and uncles had played in years before. Discarded home items from past decades brought to life by imagination. Bedsprings for the bedroom, a cupboard for the pantry and an old wood stove where numerous mud pies were made, even a discarded toilet bowl to allow us to have indoor plumbing. We used sticks to draw lines on the ground for walls and pulled weeds to make our house larger. A tree was the knocking post and entry door. Sometimes we swung on the sack swing that hung from a large cottonwood. With an extra push, we were spinning and holding on for dear life. We got wet in the creek, and the hay mound was the hideout from the little cousins not big enough to climb the ladder. We stayed warm jumping around on the bales of hay in the winter.

"Go make your own fun" was definitely a way to get us kids out from underfoot of the adults. It was understandable, with only a few rooms to hold the ever-growing family that started with Oma, Opa and their twelve children. And truth be told, even if we were initially disappointed that we were cast off to leave the adults alone, when it was time to leave we had by then made our own fun and really didn't want to go.

"Make your own fun" is not a concept lost through the years. I find great joy hearing a cousin, now a parent, tell their children to go off and make their own fun. Just as I told my children as they were growing up.

Making your own fun is a skill. It is also an attitude. I like to say, "I always have fun, sometimes more fun than other times." I am not being flippant. I truly believe that having fun is a choice. We all get to choose. It comes down to a decision and a gentle nudge.

A key to making your own fun is knowing what fun is to you. Perhaps you would like to try a measure of planned spontaneity. To practice the "Make Your Own Fun" muscle, write a list of fun things you would like to do. Anything and everything that pops into your head, write it down. Keep this list with you for a week, adding to it as more and more ideas come to you—and they will. Add solo adventures and activities to enjoy with friends or family. Add ideas that are free as well as extravagant. Add ideas that are a minute or two of fun and some that are a whole day or longer. This is not the time for common sense, practical thinking, and frugality. Rather, Make Your Own Fun is expansive and limitless!

If time in your schedule opens up and something fun has not made itself known to you, look at your list. Pick something and go Make Your Own Fun.

One more tip: You do not have to wait passively for your calendar to tell you, "You have open time, please schedule fun." Make it a priority to schedule fun as a part of your day, and Make Your Own Fun.

Balance

❧

"The life of this world is nothing but the harmony of opposites."

—RUMI

I used to try for a balanced life. The kind of life that could be plotted into a pie chart, symmetrically filling all the wedges of the circle at any point in time. But it was bullshit. I had hoped for mornings that started off with sunshine and birds singing while the family smiled at breakfast. Where everything was organized and ready for the day. A work day where all issues were easily and quickly handled, and all went smoothly. Appointments easily kept because there was only one event happening at a time. Homemade meals on the table with placemats, napkins and candles, without any whiny comments like *"I don't want that for supper."* I had visions of perfectly kept bedtime schedules, children in their own beds, teeth brushed, tucked in only once with a bedtime story and snuggles. My fantasy was only that, a fantasy.

In reality, I was balancing how to get kids home from different events at different locations at the exact same time while also attending a volunteer meeting and hubby was at work. In reality, I was balancing how not to freak out when the dog puked on the carpet five minutes before a client arrived. In reality, I was trying not to cry when I was exhausted, wanting only to sleep, and a small voice would call out, "Mom, can I have another drink of water?"

For many of us, we find an early example of balance at the playground on the teeter totter, the long board with a fulcrum in the middle. When one side goes up, the other goes down. It can be lots of fun when two evenly matched people are on either end, when the activities of our life ebb and flow in conjunction with each other. Then the teeter totter works in a fun and fluid manner: push up, glide down, push up, glide down … balance in the middle for a while and then return to an up and down playful movement.

Life is not a collection of events that only go up and down. Life flows in and around the spaces of our lives. Static balance when the teeter totter is sitting in the middle can be a nice reprieve from the crazy pace of life. It doesn't happen often. Mostly it happens right after a critical mass has just exploded, and in the aftermath we imagine that there is balance. It does not typically last long, but gives us a space to catch our breath. Having the ability to move up and down, yet sometimes get off the teeter totter and have moments of stillness—this is the best of balance.

It is easy to desire that static balance space, sitting on the teeter totter as if you are just floating in air with the feeling that all is right with the world and your life. But life can seem more like the bully three years older and bigger than you, unbalancing you on the other side of the teeter totter. Life seems to push up so hard that you slam into the ground and get jolted at the hard stop. Then up you go, holding on for dear life as the stop at the top nearly sends you flying off into the air. And just when you think you are in the center, ready for the balance in the middle, you realize that it is just the bully with his longer legs holding you up in the air, robbing you of the ability to move up or down. You are stuck.

What if we shift from striving for the perfection of balance? Searching in life for the experiences that mimic that perfect teeter totter playdate or running away from the big kid on the teeter totter. What about connecting with the flow and movement of life? It might be getting off the teeter totter and hanging on the monkey bars for a while, or taking on a new adventure and going down the slide. The desire of balance in our lives can cloud the fact that life happens in the ups and downs and spins around the merry-go-round.

REFLECTION

What is the one thing that, if you had more of it in your life, would increase your satisfaction? Write it down. Then think of other things that would also increase your satisfaction, and write those down, too. Write down as many things as come to you.

Pick the most important. Next, consider the steps you need to bring this into reality. Think baby steps. Just for today, take one tiny step towards this goal.

We may never have a balanced life, but may we have more moments that make life memorable and sweet.

Junior High Love

❧

*"May the road rise to meet you, may the wind be always
at your back, may the sun shine warm upon your face,
the rains fall soft upon your fields and, until we meet again,
may God hold you in the palm of his hand."*

—Traditional Irish blessing

When I was in junior high I was in love. He was a senior, handsome with short blond wavy hair, and dimples, and the best smile, and ooh so funny. He was also anything but interested. I was an annoying junior high girl in the same class as his brother. Any time he was near me, my heart fluttered and my cheeks flushed. His lack of attention did not diminish my love, admiration or junior high giddiness.

In our small rural community, grades 7-12 were held in one building. The border between junior high students and senior high students was defined by what time you ate lunch. Unless you were a senior—in which case you had a senior lounge: a room with a couch and comfy chairs. Going to a school in one building gave me the opportunities to brush past upperclassmen in the hall, on special occasions such as pep rallies or sports games, or even on the bus. Or when your seventh-grade English class is producing a school paper, and it is your responsibility to volunteer to interview the seniors on their future plans and best memories of school. I had a wonderful time walking in the halls, looking for those elusive seniors with all their swag. I was even given exclusive access to the "senior lounge" for some of the interviews. This was the holy grail of assignments as far as I was concerned.

Graduation came, the seniors moved on, but my junior high love for that one particular senior persisted.

And then he died. By suicide. I was in ninth grade.

That afternoon, my parents called me out of my room where I was doing homework. I walked into the living room with its brown carpet and well-worn furniture. Both my mom and dad were in the living room—which was not odd in itself, but given how they were standing, how they both looked at me with sadness, I knew something had happened. In our rural farming community, generations of families were neighbors and friends. Sadness and heartache were shared. This was certainly the case when a family who lived just down the road lost a son.

After revealing the circumstances of my summons to the living room, my parents wanted to know if I was okay. What could I say? They didn't know that the love of my life was just whisked away. I felt like I as in a trance, hearing but not hearing, not in control of my own movements as I returned to my room, shut the door and sat at my student desk made of pressed wood and peeling paper finish.

I had a cassette player on top of the desk, and I put in a tape of the B-52s. Their album *Bouncing Off the Satellites* was one of my favorites. I played the tape from the beginning. I heard one of the songs, "Communicate," as if it were the first time. I hit stop. Rewind. Again and again... *Let loose... Before it causes problems.... and it tears you apart... You gotta reach out... Communicate....Before it's too late....Talk from your heart and not just your brain.*

Crying, sobbing and asking *why?*, I didn't understand. I didn't understand his choice. I didn't understand my own feelings. I didn't understand anything.

But I knew. I knew the feeling of sadness and desperation when you want something to be different than it is. I knew others were affected by his choice. I knew that this one action had ripples out into the world. The pain bounced around my fifteen-year-old head and heart looking for the space of understanding.

We were allowed to miss school for the funeral. We walked the five blocks to the church. I felt very alone. The feelings of admiration and giddiness from just a few months ago were now such sadness. I didn't want to sit by the other students in my class. I didn't want them to see how devastated I was or see me crying if I couldn't stop myself during the service. I gave my classmate a hug, not knowing what it feels like to lose a brother. I had no words except "I'm sorry." During the service I didn't cry. I don't even think I was there. I was remembering times on the bus, at school, working in the bean fields, meaningful minuscule interactions that flooded my mind. I walked slowly back to school that day watching my feet on the sidewalk, with the words from the song playing in my mind on repeat. *Let loose... Before it causes problems... and it tears you apart... You gotta reach out... Communicate... Before it's too late... Talk from your heart and not just your brain.*

REFLECTION

Questions after a suicide or other tragedy never fill the void. Answers are never enough. Family landscapes change forever. When there are no words meaningful enough to mend the shattered heart, I choose to say a loving kindness meditation/prayer.

This loving kindness prayer begins with the focus on yourself. Just as in an airplane, you must put on your own air mask. Finding a sense of peace always starts within, then we expand and include others.

May I be filled with loving kindness.
May I be safe from inner and outer dangers.
May I be well in body and mind.
May I be at ease and happy.

May you be filled with loving kindness
May you be safe from inner and outer dangers.
May you be well in body and mind.
May you be at ease and happy.

May all beings be filled with loving kindness.
May all beings be safe from inner and outer dangers.
May all beings be well in body and mind.
May all beings be at ease and happy.

Coach

ॐ

*"There is no passion to be found settling for a life that is
less than the one you are capable of living."*

—Nelson Mandela

The decision to do something you have never done before, not knowing what the outcome will be, takes courage. It takes effort to start a new adventure that you feel like you want to, or even need to.

Like coaching Saturday morning soccer. We lived in a small community and the soccer program was parent-run, all volunteers. Gabby, my oldest, played soccer for a couple of years, and I used the excuse of my non-existent soccer knowledge to opt out of volunteering. Then it was time for our youngest, Ariel, to start. Each year, the program sent us a form that asked what positions of helpfulness you would like to assist with. This time, I decided that coaching seven-year-olds in their first year of soccer was something I could handle. I was going to be at the soccer fields anyway, and the veteran coaches assured me that the ability to give encouragement was the number-one goal. I was totally up for that. My job was to encourage them to play their positions on offense or defense, and tell them not to all run toward the ball at the same time, watch where the ball was kicked instead of visiting with the other players, kick the ball toward the goal or a team mate, and shout out the ever-present cheer of "Run!"

Soccer was a success. I felt confident in my stretching to try something new, coaching kids to play, have fun and enjoy being outside.

When my daughter's seventh-grade traveling volleyball team needed a coach, I considered stepping up. My husband thought I was a little off my rocker. "What do you know about coaching volleyball?" he wondered. I knew nothing, but wanted to learn. "But why do you want to do *this*?" he asked.

"Because they've said the season will be cancelled if someone doesn't step forward," I told him. "A whole team of girls would miss out on an opportunity. I want our daughter—who is very excited to be with her friends and wants to play volleyball—to be able to do that."

I got books from the library about coaching volleyball and read the packet given out by the association from front to back. Still, I lost sleep over my volunteering gig. I had never coached volleyball. I hadn't even played it in decades. What was I trying to prove? Then I realized: I wasn't trying to prove anything. I had the same philosophy for coaching the seventh-grade girls as the seven-year-olds. I would encourage them to do their best and have fun. I believed the point was not to win at all costs but to give all members of the team a chance to play, to practice fundamentals, and, of course, to celebrate successes.

I had to internalize my own philosophy as well. As a coach, you had to referee a certain number of games per tournament. I wanted to faint and throw up the first time I had to start a game as referee. My mouth was dry as I blew my whistle to start the game. It was a place of vulnerability. What if I did it wrong? What if I made a mistake and missed a call or called a point for the wrong team? All those what-ifs happened. I completely missed where the ball landed so I didn't know who should get the point and had to call a redo. I missed calls, and made wrong calls. And

I chose to keep going and show myself some compassion and give it another try, because all the girls were watching. They were taking it all in. They noticed when I was calm on the sidelines after an unfortunate call or play, and when I cheered a good play. They noticed when I hooted and hollered when a girl did something she had been practicing and it worked. They also saw me rotate in players in a consistent and regular way, because playing and learning was more important to me than winning.

When I was coaching, I never expressed dissatisfaction about how the girls played. They were on the floor, trying and learning. I do not believe that anyone had the right to judge that.

In the end, I gained more than I thought by trying this coaching thing. I was able to practice self-compassion. I stretched into a place of not knowing and I survived.

REFLECTION

Starting something new can feel like a stretch. It can take you out of your comfort zone. This is the place to take some time for self-compassion. What would it be like if you started every new experience with compassion? Explore the possibilities with the following exercise:

Feel your feet on the floor. Take a slow breath or two. Now give yourself a little pep talk. What compassionate things would you say to a dear friend ready to embark on a new adventure? Say those kind and compassionate things to yourself. Say them out loud. Or write them down and read them to yourself for an ongoing source of encouragement.

This exercise can be used in many situations, not just when you are starting something new. Explore all the times you can use the embrace of kindness and compassion and then give it to yourself.

Memories

"A house is made of walls and beams;
a home is built with love and dreams."

—WILLIAM ARTHUR WARD

We had made our house a home over eighteen years. We filled it with love and laughter, dogs and daughters, friends and family, dreams and many memories. We were relocating away from this home because of a job change for hubby. I started our downsizing without knowing how big our next home would be. Cleaning out closets and rooms, getting rid of stuff I had held on to for too long and things I had no idea why I was holding on to them at all. I felt good decluttering and re-homing things to family and friends and thrift stores. Both daughters had moved out and were making their own homes and taking most of their things.

It turned out our new house would be about half the size of the old one. Round two of getting rid of things began. The first round was really painless, but the second round—although not painful—took longer, as I needed to process everything a little more and take time to savor the memories. My letters from college friends written over the summer months, the boxes of projects the girls had done from preschool to high school. As these portable memories were sorted and boxed, I decided to address the thing that could not be boxed. The land.

I took a slow deliberate walk around the perimeter of our property. I was filled with gratitude for all the memories that rushed back. The place where the swing set once stood, passed on years earlier. The place where we buried the bunnies after they passed. Memories of the girls playing cops and robbers with the neighborhood kids, putting on parades with the wagon, playing house, drawing with chalk on the driveway. I shed tears of gratitude while remembering. We loved our home. The memories were now a part of our lives. I said a prayer, asking that as we left this home and took all our memories with us, that the next family would be open to sharing their love and dreams with the house and property to make it their home.

REFLECTION

Some memories can be boxed up and saved. Others, not so much. The following ritual connects you with gratitude and appreciation for the memories that cannot be boxed, such as the memory of walking the land around a house. The same ritual can also be used inside a house or any other location.

Gratitude and Letting Go Ritual:
Begin on a corner of the land to be walked. Take a few breaths. Feel the ground beneath your feet, feel the air upon your skin. Offer up a prayer of gratitude for the land, what it has given, how it has supported you and your life as a place to be. Then very slowly and deliberately walk around the perimeter of the land. With each step say "thank you." Pause anytime a memory comes back that you want to focus some attention on. Continue walking around the perimeter until complete. If there are any specific places you want to visit that are not around the perimeter, do so now,

pausing to offer up gratitude. When the walkabout is complete, pause again. Allow the breath to move in and out for a minute or two. Allow the gratitude and gifts of the land to move into your body, the memories reclaimed. You may want to finish with another prayer of gratitude and a final "thank you." The ritual is complete.

Four Scoops

❧

*"We are hard-wired to seek love, joy, fulfillment—
and health. Though we've too often been talked out of our
desires as children, I've learned that we can trust those feelings
that make us want to get out of bed in the morning."*

—Christiane Northrup, Women's Bodies, Women's Wisdom:
Creating Physical and Emotional Health and Healing

Kisha, my thirteen-year-old niece, came to visit. After a lazy Saturday morning in our pajamas we readied ourselves for the day and headed out to see some of the local shops. By mid-afternoon, the sun was heating up the day and we were ready for some ice cream to give us a break from the heat and window shopping.

The little ice-cream shop had a line of people waiting outside, but soon we moved into the coolness of the air conditioning. The menu board hanging behind the counter gave a dizzying array of choices. There was sugar cone, regular cone, waffle cone (in two sizes, no less!), and multiple sizes of bowls. You could add bits of sweets, chocolate, caramel … all those flavors and combinations were a recipe for choice paralysis. Complicating things even more, you could also get multiple flavors on a scoop-by-scoop basis—chocolate and vanilla and strawberry, perhaps. You might think this would make the decision easier, but for some people it multiplies the variety of choices to the nth degree. This is where dear Kisha was indecision to the max.

I remember being thirteen and the feeling of not knowing what the right choice was. I knew very well how Kisha's indecision felt. I was glad there was a line of people in front of us, taking their time to order their cool creamy treats and cones. I reassured her that she could order anything she wanted. And I meant it. I could see her wheels turning, trying to decide on the right choice. "How much will it cost? How much is too much? Did Auntie really mean order *anything*?" I wanted to give her the confidence that nothing would be a wrong choice. I was projecting what I would have loved to have known at thirteen, about choices, ice cream, and life.

It was our turn, and Kisha ordered a large waffle cone with four scoops of ice cream. A crazy amount of ice cream for any one person, and I could have purchased a gallon of ice cream for the same price. I marveled at how fast my brain jumped from supporting her young choice to this zone of judgement.

I decided to watch my thoughts as they came up. To see my thoughts with love and acceptance and to support this beautiful girl in making a decision. An amazing barrage of phrases came into my mind. The tone was so typical of the inner critic that has been in my mind for as long as I can remember.

This inner critic wanted me to spew out the same tone to Kisha. I refused. These were not words from my heart. They were words I had heard from others during my life, as well as my own inner critic.

"If you order that much ice cream you better eat it all, you don't want to waste it."

"Do you know how expensive that is?"

"I don't think you will be able to finish that all."

"Look at how much you have wasted."

"Your tummy hurts? Not surprising with all that you ate."

"I hope you can go for a walk and work off those calories."

"Eating like that will make you fat."

Every time a phrase popped into my head, I listened closely to it and was astonished at the sharpness. I saw how damaging similar phrases had been to my own heart. I could feel how much hurt they would cause another young heart if they were ever spoken. How interesting to have these thoughts play in my mind as if they belonged there. How easily they could have been spewed out on another young heart.

Kisha couldn't finish her ice cream. But I just smiled. Her ice cream decision had scooped out the stinging comments sitting in my heart, where they had been taking up space for too long. It was time to throw them out like the melted and dripping cone.

REFLECTION

For one day, pay attention to the dialogue within your head. Consciously be aware of your thoughts and pay close attention to the tone—the optimism, the pessimism, the worry or excitement, the fear or anger. Just pay attention.

In the evening, reflect on what you observed. Were the words helpful, uplifting, supportive? After observing your thoughts, would you choose different words if you were speaking them aloud? Or if the words were spoken to someone else?

Tomorrow, once again pay attention to your inner dialogue. Without any shame, and without "shoulding" yourself, if a thought comes in that is not helpful, that you wouldn't dare utter to another soul, stop. Renovate the unhelpful thought into one that is kinder and more helpful. Have compassion with yourself, and remind yourself that this is practice. It's all just practice, and we just keep practicing.

Grace and Ease

&

"May today there be peace within.
May you trust that you are exactly where you
are meant to be at this moment.
May you not forget the infinite possibilities that are within you.
May you be content knowing you are a child of the Creator."

—ATTRIBUTED TO TERESA OF AVILA

My friend Sue and I met through Sue's mother, Mary Jane, a hospice patient who was too stubborn to rely on her oxygen machine as continuously as she perhaps needed to. She was a spunky, petite Irish woman who was already in hospice when I meet her as one of my massage therapy clients. Sue tells the story that she used to give her mother foot massages, but lost the job after I started coming to see her mother. Mary Jane would say, "Thanks dear, but Tanya can do that when she comes this week, and she does it better."

Months after the death of Mary Jane, Sue asked to meet for lunch. During lunch we reminisced about Mary Jane's determination and stubbornness and sass. Sue asked me if I would be interested in providing massages during a retreat she was planning. I appreciated her thinking of me, and I told her I would think about it. I was a little taken aback, because I too had thought about leading a retreat or workshop. I wasn't sure what I wanted it to look like. But here was someone I could totally work with and co-create this spark of an idea. Later, I told her that instead of merely doing massages at a retreat, I was very interested in working together to plan something new. She agreed.

We met at Sue's house to connect and see what ideas we could come up with. Sitting quietly, we connected with our breath, letting there be a space of being. We both said that we felt Mary Jane was there with us, smiling that she brought us together. Our retreat, "Living with Grace and Ease," was born—the very first of many we would work on together.

We decided that we would love to have five women attend our retreat, but realized that even if no one signed up, the effort would still be a success. It was worth it for the work we had put forth, the material we put together, and the time we spent getting to know each other as dear friends. We each had a desire to share with women that life doesn't have to be a struggle. That the stories we tell our selves and our reactions to them can take away the peace that can be in our lives. There is a saying that we teach what we most need to learn. And for us it was true: Sue and I were really just gathering the information that we needed to incorporate more fully into our own lives.

We knew that the women who would be interested in "Living with Ease and Grace" would have busy schedules. We wanted the event to be fun and the day to be short enough that those that wanted to come could find the time. Our rented meeting space had plenty of chairs. The tiny kitchen in back was perfect for the coffee, tea and fruit we planned to serve.

After announcing the retreat and hoping for a good turnout, we were astonished when 18 women signed up. Gulp ... so much for just doing the work for ourselves. We polished up our presentation, determined to share ideas, tips and tools to help women bring ease and grace into their lives.

The women who came for that morning retreat shared from their hearts, graciously took what we had to share, amped up the fun with some dancing, and were genuinely disappointed when the morning was done.

After we said goodbye to the last woman, Sue and I took time to let the success of the day wash over us. We were so grateful for how the women we met had shared and reflected back to us what we wanted to accomplish. We wanted women to take some time for themselves, to be themselves, and to be in a circle where they could be supported and loved. Sue and I in turn had that same experience. Not only with the group that lovely Saturday morning, but also with each other during our planning sessions.

Sue and I went on to be dear friends and co-creators of many workshops, retreats, and women's circles. Hosting our very first was a practice in letting things be easy, graceful, and fun. It was a practice in taking gentle action, much like the relationship Sue and I had—with the help of Mary Jane, of course.

REFLECTION

It is not just in the big moments that we desire and see grace and ease—many times it is in the smallest. The moments that are easy to miss if we are not paying attention. The slipping of the sun below the horizon or the gentle rising of the sun in the distance. The dewdrops on a petal or the smell of a spring blossom. The moon illuminating the landscape or a fall leaf floating to the ground. A hug from a dear one, a call from someone special.

The abundance of grace and ease in our lives is illumined by awareness. Some days, life feels like an ocean giving us grace and ease, wave after wave. Other times, it feels as though we are in a desert and the waves of grace are only memories. These are the times to pause, and look at the snippets of life that fall to the wayside, the pieces that are easily overlooked.

Where do you find grace and ease reflected back to you in life? Make a list. Add to it, and refer back to it. Allow grace and ease to be your intention and then put your attention upon it and watch it grow.

Timing

❧

"You may delay, but time will not."

—Benjamin Franklin

The roads were an icy disaster. I had already postponed a hospice massage appointment until later morning, hoping that the sun would melt the ice from the highways on the fifty-four-mile round trip. I drove slowly over roads that were mostly iced over, leaving only sparse patches of clear pavement. The trip was slow but uneventful. The massage left the client relaxed and sleeping, and I readied myself to leave.

I was chatting briefly with Michelle, the hospice client's caregiver, when the client's husband, Mark, came into the kitchen after raking snow off the roof. Mark had a great sense of humor. After I made a joke and he didn't respond, I thought he was kidding me by making a snoring sound. But then he didn't respond to my witty comeback—and the snoring sound stopped. Michelle looked perplexed, and we both moved toward Mark.

In a CPR class, they assure you that you will know what to do and remember the steps when an emergency happens. I was amazed at all the information that jumped into my brain. The videos during class had seemed silly, watching someone holler, "Are you alright? Can you hear me?" But that was exactly what I did. Panic rose along with the volume of my voice: "Mark! Mark!

Are you all right? *Can you hear me?!*" I shook his shoulder, willing him to respond. He didn't seem to be breathing.

Mark was sitting on a kitchen chair with rollers, and Michelle and I moved him to the floor. Mark was a tall man, close to 200 pounds. It was not a gentle, soft transition. As we pulled him off the chair, it rolled and his head hit the floor with a decisive thud. We both checked to see if he was breathing, and to see if we could feel a pulse. Nothing. Michelle and I looked at each other, eyes wide with disbelief. "'We should start CPR," Michelle said.

"I'll call 911."

Michelle started compressions. I got up and moved to grab the phone. Dialing with shaking hands, I stammered to the dispatcher that we needed an ambulance. The dispatcher asked for the address, and I paused for what felt like several minutes. I didn't know. I had been coming so regularly that I didn't remember the address anymore.

"What's the address, Michelle?" I asked urgently. She told me, but my mind couldn't grasp the information quickly enough to repeat it. I handed the phone to Michelle and let her talk. While she spoke with the dispatcher, I continued with CPR. When you do compressions correctly, you press hard enough to separate the sternum from the cartilage. This makes a cracking sound, after which there is more space within the body for the compressions to do the job of moving blood from the heart.

The dispatcher let us know a sheriff's deputy and an ambulance would be on the way, but that with the roads being so icy, their arrival could be longer than expected.

Mark had turned grey and his lips were blue. He looked much worse than he had a minute ago. We continued with CPR. Michelle started compressions. Fifteen compressions to two breaths were the latest teaching. I started with breaths. I knew that you were supposed to use a mouth shield to protect from the passing on of diseases. I didn't have one, and made the choice to go ahead anyway. Tilt the head. Pinch the nose. Stop compressions. Breathe one, breathe two. Continue compressions. Again, tilt head. Pinch the nose. This time I couldn't make a seal around Mark's mouth with my own. His dentures had come loose and were sitting in his mouth. I put my fingers in his mouth, and fished for the dentures, which were covered in mucus, to pull them out. I placed them up on the table. It was difficult to continue. I grabbed a napkin off the table, wiped the mucus off my mouth—and as much mucus as I could out of his mouth—and then I did more breaths.

The ambulance had more than ten miles to drive on icy roads. The ambulance crew is voluntary—so when dispatch sends out a page to the crew, it takes a few minutes for them to get to the ambulance garage and head to where they're needed. We knew we would be doing CPR for a while.

A deputy sheriff arrived at the house with a AED—an automated external defibrillator—used to shock a person's heart. The deputy moved over to Mark as we unbuttoned his shirt, and placed the sticker pads that would administer the shock. One on the right side above the nipple and the other on the left side below the breast, all very simply demonstrated on the AED equipment. When the deputy pressed the shock button, the AED analyzed Mark's condition and determined that it could not shock him. The deputy tried again. The AED still wouldn't go, and indicated that we should continue CPR.

The ambulance crew arrived. "Move out of our way, please", they said as the crew of three came quickly into the kitchen. We picked ourselves off the floor and stepped back. Efficiently moving Mark onto the stretcher, out the door, and into the ambulance, soon they were gone.

Quiet. Hearts racing. Heads spinning. Time was not real. How long had it been since I said goodbye, but didn't leave? Then I remembered: The hospice client! Mark's wife had been in the living room through all the commotion—all that activity, all that coming and going. Worried about how this was all affecting her, we checked on her. She was still sleeping. Her disease, a blessing during this ordeal, seemed to keep her unaware of what had just happened.

Adrenaline shot through our systems, and Michelle and I took our racing hearts and shaking hands and tried to drink some water. We rehashed the last 30 minutes. What we remembered and what we didn't remember.

That evening I met a dear friend and related the shock of the day's events to her. It felt surreal, like I was describing a movie. I didn't have a lot of hope that our actions had been enough to save Mark's life.

Epilogue: Although Mark was transferred to a larger hospital, he never regained consciousness before he passed away.

REFLECTION

Synchronicities, being in the right place at the right time, happenstance, coincidences, divine timing, grace. No matter what you call it, there are circumstances that do not seem to have an explanation.

The phrase "it is what it is" comes to mind. What happened is more important than why it happened. The *what ifs* are then replaced with the gratitude of *what was* because what could have been, could have been worse.

Sometimes it can be best to connect with the here and now. Use the following practice to do so.

Take a moment to get comfortable. Allow the breath to be the focus. Feel the breath move in and out of your body. Your eyes may be open or closed. Allow your shoulders to relax away from your ears. Feel your feet on the floor, your seat on the chair. The breath is moving in and out naturally and relaxed. Place one or two hands on your heart center. Continue with the relaxed breath and repeat slowly, "I am here now... I am here now... I am here now." Releasing your hands, continue focusing on the breath until you feel complete.

Downtown

ॐ

"I'm an idealist. I don't know where I'm going, but I'm on my way."

—CARL SANDBURG

My younger brother had an appointment with an ear specialist in downtown Minneapolis, with its population of over 350,000 people. I was 17 and highly capable of navigating the streets of the big city—or so I thought. I had grown up in the country, on a farm five miles from the nearest town, and that town had a whopping 500 residents. How difficult could it be to walk down a city street?

As we entered the office building that housed the doctor's office, my parents told me to meet back in this exact place in 45 minutes. I was ready to shake off the parents and little brother and explore. I had a lovely time window-shopping and people-watching, and before I knew it, it was time to make my way back. I went into what I thought was the correct office building. It looked exactly like the one I had left earlier. Examining the office directory, I didn't see the doctor's name. That was a surprise. I was sure I was in the right place. But, I thought, maybe I was confused because I had crossed the street while walking around. I went across the street to another building that looked exactly the same. I checked that roster of tenants—nope, still not the correct building. My nervousness grew as I realized I was going to be late.

I was anxious about how my parents would react. But I had no other option than to take some deep breaths and keep looking.

I went back to the sidewalk and continued to walk down the street, intently looking at each building, willing them to tell me which one was the right one. At one point, I thought I heard my name. But when I looked around, I didn't see anyone. I must have been hearing things. Turning the corner, I kept walking and looking for the elusive building. I wasn't panicking, but I knew I was going to have to think of another way to find my family rather than just walking the downtown streets. Just then I walked by a building that I hadn't checked yet, or so I thought, and my mom pushed open the door and yelled "Tanya!" I was grateful and relieved to have found my family—and to be found. My mother had some sharp words which I, being 17, automatically took personally, and which electrified my wall of teenage sullenness and vaporized all my gratitude.

After sharpening my street-smart savviness through this experience, I started to feel more confident about navigating the big city. A few months later, I drove with my girlfriends to Minneapolis for a day of theater and fun.

Thirty years later, a conversation between my mother and I brought back the memory of being lost in Minneapolis. "My heart is racing just thinking about it," my mother told me as she explained her perspective of what had happened. "We were just about ready to call the cops!" As it turned out, that mysterious voice I'd heard calling my name on the crowded street had been my mother, although I could not see her. She told me how her heart had dropped as I disappeared around the corner. She had scolded herself, wishing she had told me the building's address before letting me walk away and explore.

I assured my mother that I did not have any lingering trauma and encouraged her to let go of hers as well, because I was alright. I promised not to get lost again.

My father had also been along on our Minneapolis foray, but his memory was much different. In fact, when I asked him about it years later, he didn't remember that I had been lost at all! No recollection, no trauma. Your story is your story. Some stories we remember only that they happened, some stories are associated with stress or trauma, and there are plenty of stories we don't remember at all.

REFLECTION

Trauma is not in the event. It is the nervous system's response to the event. You can see this in the way my mother, father, and I all had different ways of remembering the day I got lost. None of us were wrong. It's just that we all had our own story, and our own memory of the experiences, to help us gauge what had happened.

To question someone else's experience of trauma is to assume that you know all the paths they have walked. We can't. What we can do is look at our own experiences with compassion. We can acknowledge that we may have specific emotions attached to an event. Not all trauma affects our day-to-day life. Some prior traumas can be looked at through the lens of time and compassion. Other traumas may need professional help to wade through. If you have a prior trauma that is disrupting your current life, I urge you to find professional help.

Mother's Day

&

"Life is what happens to us while we are making other plans."

—ALLEN SAUNDERS

I began my very first Mother's Day weekend in the hospital, on the edge of life.

I loved being pregnant. The thickness and growth of my hair from the prenatal vitamins. The glow of growing another human inside my own body. The kind, sincere inquiries and overt gestures of helpfulness from strangers: *"Can I help you with that? Can I get you anything? Please let me get the door for you."* The overall feeling of being treated like a queen. The first three months of morning sickness were rough, especially when lasted past the morning and into the afternoon and night. But it eased up as I moved past the first trimester. Towards the end of my last trimester, I had a few pangs of pain in my chest. It lasted for only a few minutes, but was significant enough for me to mention it to my doctor, who dismissed it as just heartburn and told me it would likely go away after I gave birth. I wasn't sure—it didn't *feel* like any heartburn I had ever experienced—but I pushed away the thought that it could be something else. This was prior to the existence of online resources like webMD, so any further research to diagnose myself wasn't even on my radar. If the doctor said it was heartburn, then maybe it was only heartburn.

Soon enough I was a mother and had my hands full taking care of a newborn.

I went back to work after my eight-week maternity leave was up. One afternoon, just a week or so later, I had shooting pains in my chest, stabbing pain that shot through to my back, taking my breath with it. It hurt so substantially that I couldn't talk through the pain, couldn't stand up straight, couldn't catch my breath. I moved into the restroom down the hall from my desk, inhaling tiny shallow breaths, my arm outstretched with my hand on the bathroom wall, holding myself up. Whenever the pain subsided enough for me to stand upright, another wave would come and I would double over again, willing the pain to recede. The episode eventually passed and when I could take moderately full breaths again, I went back to my desk and finished the workday, hoping the worst was over. When I had another episode with the same intensity of pain, I decided to see my doctor. After an ultrasound, I was diagnosed with gallstones.

I met with a surgeon, Dr. White, who helped me understand my illness. He explained where the gallbladder was, how it functioned, why the gallstones were causing pain, and what was involved in removing my gall bladder and gallstones. I learned what to expect from the laparoscopy, a procedure where three small incisions are made so that the gallbladder can be taken out with minimal time in the hospital and a quicker recovery. This procedure was scheduled for the following week.

But my body decided that it did not want to follow the surgery schedule, and was looking for a quicker resolution. The following morning, I felt horrible. I hadn't been able to keep any food down. I had felt sick while I had been up during the night breastfeeding our two-month-old daughter, and I was in an extreme amount of pain from what I now knew was an acute gallbladder attack. When my husband arrived home from working the night shift, I asked him to take me to the doctor.

One look from the doctor, and I was told to go to the hospital. Soon I was being prepped for surgery. Apparently, turning yellow from jaundice plus a blood test showing a very unhappy liver is a surefire way get a gallbladder laparoscopy rescheduled to the very next available operating room.

While I waited for the hospital to finalize paperwork, my eyes were tightly squeezed in pain. I was amazed that this sharp, searing feeling was more intense than what I had felt during childbirth just two months earlier. I hadn't taken any pain medication then, yet now I was begging for something, *anything* to help. At last, though, it kicked in and I could relax and rest before it was time for surgery.

My husband is a nurse, and as he waited alone for me he knew that each minute that ticked past the doctor's predicted completion time meant something had not gone as planned. Being in the medical field gives you an insight that is not always comforting. After more than twice the expected time went by, the surgeon emerged from the operating room to give him a report. There was a slight alteration to the surgical plan, he said, but assured my husband that everything was fine.

The laparoscopic technique to remove my gallbladder had been unsuccessful, so the surgeon needed to do a more invasive procedure called an open cholecystectomy to find the gallstones that had migrated out of the gallbladder. In addition to three one-inch incisions for the laparoscopy, I would now need a ten-inch incision diagonally across my torso, closed as neatly as surgical staples allow. "Fine" in my case was a relative term, one meant to ease my family's worry and sidestep any further conversation. "Fine," in this case, meant "alive, for now."

"This can't be good," was the thought that came to me when I woke up. I lay in a hospital bed, unaware of the exact time, but it was late, the night-shift nurses well into their duties. I couldn't move anything but my eyelids, which I opened tiredly and briefly but then shut again. I was overcome with fatigue and the after-effects of anesthesia and surgery. As a nurse checked my vitals, I heard her and my anesthesiologist discuss my current state of health, or lack thereof, with strict instructions to to call him immediately at home if there was any change in my condition.

The day after surgery, I drifted in and out of awareness, not knowing even what day of the week it was. I had visitors, and I remember trying to stay awake. I remember their looks of concern, and how they cut their visits short to let me rest because I would drift off while they were talking to me.

I didn't know how sick I was or even that there was something wrong with me other than normal post-surgery recovery. Nurses and doctors came and went. They encouraged me to cough and sit up in bed, all of which seemed torturous. My abdomen hurt whenever I moved. My coughing caused pain in my abdomen and chest. I felt dizzy when I sat up. All the interventions meant to help my continued recovery felt like personal torture. I still felt miserable, but the pain had changed. It was not the stabbing, sharp pain that had been there when I came into the hospital, but an all-over lethargy and pain from the incisions and drain tubes. The altered surgical plan had resulted in an excessive volume of fluid in my body, which in turn led to ARDS (Acute Respiratory Distress Syndrome) and pneumonia, further adding to my pain and discomfort.

ARDS can be very serious. It happens when the alveoli, the tiny sacs in the lungs that exchange oxygen, fill with fluid. The fluid keeps the lungs from filling with enough air, which means less oxygen reaches the bloodstream. This deprives the organs of the oxygen they need to function. While pneumonia is an infection that can be cleared with antibiotics, ARDS is treated with diuretics to try and dry up the fluid. The mortality rate of a patient diagnosed with ARDS is near 50 percent.

It wasn't until much later, when I saw a picture of me holding my daughter on our first Mother's Day together, that I realized how close a call I'd had. The picture, taken two days after surgery, could be described as death warmed over—grey with a slight undertone of life.

Be your own advocate. Honor your own knowing, gain information and knowledge, and do not give away your power. If necessary, you can transfer your power to someone you trust—you can accept help, make decisions, and change your mind.

I shut down my knowing because someone I thought knew better, the doctor, told me I didn't know what it felt like to be in my body. Although neither the surgery nor my physical healing afterwards may have had a different outcome, there definitely would have been less hurt and emotional trauma had I known I could trust myself.

Trusting yourself is a practice, one that we have been taught is not sufficient. Use the following exercise to strengthen your ability to trust yourself.

Follow your breath. On the in-breath think or say out loud "I can be trusted," or "I trust myself." Whichever resonates most. On the out-breath say or think "I am trusted in the world," or "those I love can trust me." Again, whichever feels most resonant. Repeat numerous times, allowing the body to be relaxed and the breath to be even.

Getting Home

"You are not a mess. You are a feeling person in a messy world."

—GLENNON DOYLE MELTON

Transitioning from being a sick person who must stay in the hospital to a healthier sick person who can go home from the hospital is a process. Little steps towards progress feel like huge wins, and setbacks feel devastating. Going to the bathroom? Hooray! Spiking a fever? Boo. Having some postpartum blues before urgent gallbladder surgery was manageable, but it took a toll on me the longer I lay in the hospital bed, too sick to take care of my two-month-old baby girl when I yearned to be home with my family.

If not for the ARDS (Acute Respiratory Distress Syndrome), I would have spent a couple of nights in the hospital before returning to the comfort of my own home to recover. The treatment for ARDS was a diuretic to reduce excess fluid so my lungs could recover. This also meant that any milk I may have been able to produce for breastfeeding would be stripped away as well. However, I was not aware of these things. I was a young mom with undiagnosed postpartum depression. I was in pain, and not cognizant of what was even wrong with me after surgery. Even if I had been told what medication I was being given, I wouldn't have known what it was for.

I went in for surgery on a Friday. By Monday, I started asking when I could go home. Maybe Wednesday, they said. I was bolstered to get through another day and night at the hospital by visits from family and my newborn daughter. Though I was happy to see my husband and daughter in the evening, their visits were a double-edged sword, as I knew they would have to go home and I would be alone.

I was worried about being able to continue breastfeeding. My daughter was only two months old, and I had great expectations of nursing her for months longer. I thought if I could pump, I would have enough milk supply when I got home on Wednesday. This was naiveté.

The nurse brought me a hand breast pump and set it on the table by my bed. I struggled to use it. It was hard to get the right placement on my body, and I still wasn't strong enough to walk to the bathroom by myself, much less hand-pump breast milk. I wasn't aware that the diuretic medication had completely stripped my mammary glands dry. I didn't have enough awareness or confidence to use my voice and ask for help. I was devastated.

I wish that the staff would have explained my medical situation more clearly. How I needed the diuretic to bring down my excess fluid, taking pressure off my lungs, heart, and other organs, but decreasing my ability to produce breast milk. Instead, I internalized a crushing feeling of not being *enough*. I wasn't disciplined enough to do what was best for my daughter, or good enough to be home caring for her. I was just not good enough for anything.

Nine days in the hospital. My uncle, who had a heart attack a month earlier, had only stayed for three days. My last stop before going home was to pick up a prescription. The pharmacist raised an eyebrow, telling me that the prescribed dosage was usually only given to patients still staying in the hospital. But I knew that going home was better for my mental health. Lucky me! I was on my way home.

I took the time to rewrite what I wished had happened at the hospital. It gave me clarity on what I truly would have liked to be different. Did it change what happened in the past? No. But it did change the way I felt about it. I encourage you to choose a time in your life when something didn't go the way you wanted. Rewrite your story. What would you have wanted to happen? What would you have said or done differently? Take your time. Make revisions. Keep on rewriting until you feel it is complete. Do this with a great amount of self-compassion.

The Easter Bunnies

❧

"Tradition: The handing down of information, beliefs, and customs by word of mouth or by example from one generation to another without written instruction."

—Merriam-Webster Dictionary

Traditions are so interesting. Being part of a large extended family that loves tradition, I have been able to watch traditions grow and morph and experience hiccups.

One longstanding tradition in my family is the Easter Bag Hunt. I am sure my grandparents did not foresee that hiding candy on Easter Sunday would morph into the grand and colossal event that now spans five generations and includes individually labeled Easter bags for more than seventy-five family members.

When my mother was a young girl, my grandparents would hide candy outside in little bags with each child's name written on them. Why the names? To make it fair. My mom is one of twelve siblings, with an age span of twenty years from youngest to oldest. With that many children, an extra step was needed to make sure everyone received a little bit of sweets.

It was a conscious decision to include everyone and exclude no one. Traditions continue because of participation. If no one participates, the tradition dies. As our family expanded through dating, marriage and children, each new person received an Easter bag with their name on it. Aunts and uncles, cousins and grandparents would all get a bag of treats with their name. There was no opting out or sitting on the sidelines. (Though a few uncles *might* have bribed us with a cut of their treats if we found their bag for them.) But no matter what, you were going to have a bag and your name was going to be on it.

After the Easter Bunnies hid each bag, and we would all go outside at the same time for the hunt. Everyone looked around the farm for their bag, some asking for hints, some complaining the hunt was too hard, and some that it was too easy. Photos showing us wearing snow pants, hats and mittens, or short-sleeved shirts and rain boots told the tale of the weather for the day. My grandparents started this tradition of Easter bag hunts more than 65 years ago, now with so many memories a few stories that stand out.

My grandparents always parked their silver Buick Century on the east side of the house where there was an incline, next to the doghouse and the semi-circle concrete steps that led to the porch off the kitchen. One year, my uncle Loran was one of the Easter bunnies, and was finished hiding all his Easter bags except his brother Larry's. After some thought, Loran hid the bag in the right rear wheel well of the silver Buick. Loran was regularly on bunny duty, and it would be no fun if the Easter Bunny had to hide his own bag. So Larry volunteered to hide Loran's bag, and without knowing where his own bag was, hid Loran's bag in the *left* rear wheel well.

The hunt commenced, and everyone found their bags except for Loran and Larry. To help bolster the spirits of those still searching, or maybe to rub in the fact that someone else found your bag first, we'd commonly shout out, "I know where your bag is". This was the case for both Larry and Loran. Many of us had already discovered the bags in the wheel wells, but quietly replaced them so as to not spoil the fun. By this time, everyone still outside was milling around by the concrete steps. We told both Loran and Larry when they were warm or cold as they searched, but each of them very purposefully stayed away from the car—so their brother wouldn't discover *their* hiding place. They looked in the doghouse, in the flowers, next to the house—but not around the car. In the crowd, our murmuring started to turn into laughter. Someone finally said, "Look by the car."

Loran and Larry both circled around on opposite sides of the car, and looked behind the wheels. S-U-C-C-E-S-S! They lifted the bags high above their heads in victory, with the family laughing and cheering.

There have been some growing pains since the beginning of the tradition. My cousin Sarah very clearly remembers the year, when she was eight or nine, that everyone found their bag but her. After a little confusion, the aunties in charge of filling the Easter bags realized that no bag had been made for Sarah. While one auntie distracted Sarah, another did some quick magic with a marker and some masking tape. And … *tada*! "Sarah, we found your bag!"

Sarah could see clearly, though, that the bag had originally been labeled "Marlys," and knew that Aunt Marlys had given up her own bag. We did everything we could to keep the tradition positive. After this, a master list was made every year to make sure that all attendees would have a bag of their own.

One year my cousin Kristy came back up to the house after finding her Easter bag in the rock pile. The bags had been hidden hours earlier to be ready for the early-afternoon hunt. It was important to all to take inventory of the treats in your bag, so you could trade the ones you didn't like with someone else. Kristy said, "There is a hole in my bag." Upon further investigation, we discovered that the bag had been chewed through—and a critter had started eating her salted nut roll. Needless to say, next year the rock pile was off limits.

We didn't let late spring snowfalls stop us either, including the Easter I was in fifth grade. We talked about skipping the bag hunt or at least having it inside. Both ideas were squashed. We donned our winter attire and forged outside to find the bountiful bags of treats. Toward the end of the hunt, I still hadn't found my bag. The aunties doublechecked the master list and confirmed that a bag had been made. But by this year, the Easter Bunnies had close to fifty bags to hide, and the aunties had a hard time keeping track of whose bag ended up where. I had given up. No one else had even seen my bag while they were searching for their own. The Easter bunny made one more circle around the yard to jog his memory. He found it buried in the snow, completely covered and not visible at all. I was instantly relieved to have not missed out. I was disappointed that some candy was wet and ruined, but happy to have a bag and a connection to the tradition. And this led to a new part of the tradition: nowadays, the Easter bunnies carefully mark each bag on a map of the farm.

This family tradition has evolved, but the excitement and fun still continues. And we still enjoy being together in each other's company, something my grandmother instilled in us. With great pride, we choose to carry on a tradition that brings us together in the present and connects us with our past.

REFLECTION

Traditions don't have to be multigenerational family gatherings. Of course they can be shared with others, but don't limit yourself.

Traditions can carry a specialness of their own, one you shape with no one else involved, perhaps a lighting of a candle on a day that is meaningful, a walk in the woods, or a full moon.

Look at what traditions you already have in place. Check in and see if you want to expand them, give them a rest, change them or just continue to cherish them. The traditions you choose are the most meaningful.

A Gift

❧

"What the mind can conceive, it can achieve."

—Napoleon Hill

The smallest events can change the trajectory of our lives. For me it came when my mom gave me a gift certificate for an hour-long massage. Dana's Therapeutic Massage was in a neighboring town, and I had never received a massage before. I was excited to experience this relaxing gift.

I waited to make an appointment. It felt like the massage should be justified by especially sore muscles, pains and aches. It was not enough that I was a mother, working out of the house, full-time parenting two small children, and married.

On the day of my appointment, I was excited and nervous. I had only heard stories about the deep relaxation people felt with a massage. I went with expectations of feeling great afterward, but apprehensive about how I would know what I was supposed to do—or not do. The appointment started off easily enough with paperwork: the standard name and address, and then questions about past and present health, muscle discomfort, and whether I had ever received a massage before. After I'd filled out the forms, Dana, the massage therapist, asked a few clarifying questions about my main concerns.

As I moved from the reception area into the treatment room, Dana told me to undress and lie face up on the table between the sheets. Soft music played , and a glow from a lamp in the corner added to the relaxing ambiance. I quickly took off my clothes, not wanting to have the massage therapist return before I was ready. I climbed onto the massage table and covered up. "Hmmm, this is nice and warm," I thought, and I felt a comfort in the soft sheets, the weight of the blanket, the space I was giving to myself to just be.

Then tension jumped back into my mind. Did she say face up or face down? Did "take off your clothes" mean *all* of your clothes or only some? Did I answer the questions correctly on the form? Am I the tensest client she has ever had? None of these questions helped me relax.

Dana knocked and asked if I was ready. I guess I hadn't needed to hurry so much to get under the covers. Most of my questions floated out of my mind as Dana placed her warm and gentle hands on my face. She continued using a firm and gentle touch on my scalp, arms, hands, legs, and feet. Each body part was covered with the blanket or felt the gentle movement of Dana's hands erasing my tension. By the time she asked me to turn over so she could massage my back, I was so relaxed I could have drooled. My anxious questions floated away, replaced with an otherworldly feeling of relaxation. I couldn't remember a time in my life that I had felt so physically and mentally relaxed. When time was so fluid, my mind became soft and there was no striving for the next thing.

As I walked out to my car, I wondered how amazing would it be to have the skills to be able to make people feel the same way.

The gift, the massage, and the wondering all comingled and united in my mind, and changed my life. It led me to attend massage therapy school, change careers, start my own business, and connect with other people who were looking for healing hands to ease away the tension.

REFLECTION

I highly recommend getting a massage. Not because it will start a cascade of changes within your life, though it might. But because massage is a wonderful way to relax, take a pause from the stresses of life, and allow your body to receive healthy touch.

If you have never had a massage before, I believe the second massage is always more relaxing then the first. When we know what to expect, we can relax into the session even more, and gain a plethora of relaxing benefits.

Choose a trained massage therapist that makes you feel comfortable, and don't be afraid to tell the massage therapist if you want more or less pressure, or if you are too cold or too warm. Your comfort will make your appointment more successful.

Be it your first massage or your next massage, may you find the space to breathe, rest, and relax.

Wilber

❧

"In a world where you can be anything, be kind."

—Jennifer Dukes Lee

Wilber was my very first hospice massage patient. He was in his seventies and a bachelor, living in a nursing home that catered to patients with mental health diagnoses. The facility included a wing of locked units for the safety of staff, residents, and visitors. Wilber's room was on the locked side, so when I arrived, I was required to buzz in and sign a visitor log that noted my arrival and departure times. Once I'd signed the log, the staff would press the button that unlocked the door and I would pass quickly through, closing it securely behind me. After becoming a regular visitor, this process got to be quicker as staff recognized me and knew who I was visiting.

Once through the locked door, I walked down the hallway and was greeted with a rush of sensations. The smell of cleaning products that failed to mask the smell of excrement. Institutional food vapors wafting out of the kitchen along with the clanging of pans and trays. Blue-grey carpet that was thoroughly vacuumed and steamed but never completely clean. An elderly man holding onto the hallway railing and hurling the words "You no good fucking son of a bitch" at everyone and no one. My hands were cold. I was nervous to meet my new client. I continued down the hall. Wilber's room was on the left-hand side at the end of the hall, with institutional floor tile, fluorescent lights, and the drapes pulled shut. I found Wilber sitting in his wheelchair watching television news.

When a new hospice massage client was assigned to me, I would receive a client information sheet with their address, the medical diagnosis that qualified them for hospice, tidbits about their family, and sometimes a brief personal history. This helped prepare me for any special limitations that might come up during the massage, and helped me find the best way to introduce myself. Wilber's medical history listed a past diagnosis of schizophrenia, but also noted that he'd had no symptoms for a few years.

When I started doing massage therapy for hospice it was a hard sell. Massage was foreign to many people. Some had heard about it but never had received one, and others thought "massage" meant something unsavory. But the hospice social worker and nursing staff were very excited. They knew massage would be beneficial for the patients. Patients might sometimes say no initially, even though money was not the issue since the hospice program paid the fee. If that happened, hospice staff would expand their questioning to see if the patient had sore muscles or if they would like their back rubbed. Wilber wasn't sure about the idea at first, but agreed that since his shoulders and back hurt, yes, he would like to give it a try.

Meeting Wilber was a step into a career of hospice massage that I loved and performed for over ten years.

Still a bit nervous, I introduced myself: "Hi Wilber, my name is Tanya."

Wilber gave me a leery glance.

"I am here to rub your shoulders and back. Does that sound okay?"

He thought about it for a moment, then said, "Okay."

And so started our first massage session.

When our time was complete, I asked Wilber if I could come back the next week. He said yes.

Wilber and I developed an easygoing routine, and I started to be less intimidated by my surroundings when I would come for our appointment. Soon, Wilber was comfortable with me and his massage sessions too. We would chat about what was on TV while I worked on his back.

Once, a news report about Washington, D.C., came on. Wilber seemed more comfortable if we would carry on a little small talk, so I told him I had never been to D.C. but was looking forward to a trip sometime.

"Have you ever been to Washington, Wilber?" I asked.

"Yes," Wilbur said, never a man of many words.

"I hear it is lovely in the spring with all of the cherry blossoms. Did you get to see the cherry blossoms while you were in Washington?"

"'Nope. I was in a mental institution."

Gulp. "Oh," was all that I could say. I assured myself that no matter how awkward the conversation had been, knowing that Wilber had dementia, there was a good chance that he would not remember it. Not that there was anything to be ashamed of, on either of our parts. Mine for asking an innocent question, or Wilber's for living the life he lived. I am grateful for Wilber, my first hospice client, the experience of being outside my comfort zone, the ability to survive awkward conversations, and the opportunity to share caring hands.

REFLECTION

Uncomfortable situations come in a host of different sizes, but feeling awkward because of a misplaced assumption is most easily approached with compassion, humor, and a deep breath.

Assumptions are the signpost of bad intel. If we assume we know how someone feels, what they have done, what they thought, we are most often wrong. We might think we know, we might even think we know after they tell us, but we still filter the information through our own experiences and feelings. We are really good at it. We assume and make up stories all the time.

So how do we move past the trap of assumptions? By kindly asking questions and being curious. Questions are asked to clarify and show interest, and questions may also help remove judgement. Instead of assuming you know what someone wants, ask a clarifying question. When we ask clarifying questions we remove confusion. Don't let the voice in your head tell you that you will look dumb if you ask a question. That is not true. You instead become masterful at avoiding assumptions. So try asking more questions and see how easy it can be to move past assumptions and misunderstandings.

Bird Feeders

Living for more than twenty years in a small town in south central Minnesota, we had a variety of wild animals: deer, raccoons, skunks, and rabbits, to name a few. We caught sight of raccoons washing their paws in our tiny backyard pond, and rabbits were always trying to make a home under our wood pile and eating my flowers. Deer would wander through the yard, and one night the dog was sprayed by a skunk, but overall, our interactions with wildlife were pretty tame.

Then we moved to northern Minnesota and discovered things were different there. It started with my husband's habit of feeding the birds. He bought a new birdfeeder and the appropriate birdseed to hang in our wooded backyard, excited to see the different species of birds that this north country would share with us. We were curious to see if the familiar hummingbirds, Baltimore orioles, robins, and wrens would be here, and what new varieties might visit.

The night after hanging our new birdfeeder, as we were both sleeping, I awoke abruptly to the sound of crashing plastic outside our bedroom window. I tapped my husband and told him I heard a noise and thought there was something outside. Cliché, I know, but true. We jumped out of bed and squinted out into the darkness through the bedroom windows, but we couldn't see anything. There were no streetlights in the woods, and we didn't have a yard light. We moved to the living room to peer out the sliding glass door. First, we turned on the back light and all at once we saw a large figure twenty feet from the house. It moved, and we could see that it was a black bear sitting with the birdfeeder in hand, ready to have a midnight snack.

Hubby opened the sliding glass door and started to go outside. "What are you doing?" I exclaimed. "There is a bear out there!"

But my husband stepped out the sliding glass door into the backyard and shouted at the bear: "Go on! Git *outta* here!" Then he picked up a small patio table and tossed it in the bear's direction. The bear looked at us calmly, very deliberately put down the birdfeeder, and slowly waddled off into the woods—not impressed with our scariness but not inclined to make a fuss over the request to leave.

My husband, an outdoorsman, assured me that bears don't want confrontation and will just go away when encouraged to leave. Good to know! But I was still processing that real live bears could now come into my back yard like the rabbits did when we lived in town. We decided that leaving the birdfeeders out overnight was an invitation we did not want to extend.

The day after our friendly neighborhood bear came to visit, I was at the chiropractor's office and I shared the story of our bear visit with a woman waiting near me. "Oh, yes," she said, "I have to regularly chase after bears with a broom for them to leave my suet blocks alone that I put out for birds." This was definitely a shift in thinking for me. Bears were a common backyard visitor here in the north country. Their presence didn't even make an exciting story for locals, who saw them just as a fact of life.

When we shared our tales of our late-night backyard guest with family and friends outside of northern Minnesota, they reacted with astonishment, exclamations, and amazement—reactions that matched my own. They were impressed that I could be so brave to go outside anytime despite the threat of coming across a bear on my path or even just in the backyard. I assured them, with the confidence of a seasoned northerner, that black bears were docile, and even mother bears with cubs would rather avoid confrontation.

REFLECTION

Perception is an insightful action. Take some time to go outside into nature. It can be anywhere, on your patio, in your yard, by a tree, in some woods, near a puddle or a lake, a plant, a garden, anything. Observe and write down what you see. Be specific. Look for the tiny pieces that make up the whole. Write down your observations, then connect with those observations and see if any of them have a message for you.

Whether you spend five minutes or twenty-five minutes—it's through the act of observing that the magic happens.

The Next Thing

&

"You are a child of the universe no less than the trees and the stars;
you have a right to be here."

—MAX EHRMANN, "DESIDERATA"

As a child I was always wishing for the next thing. I couldn't wait until Saturday, I couldn't wait until summer vacation, I couldn't wait until the parade, I couldn't wait until Christmas, I couldn't wait until my birthday. There was always something in the future that was going to be better than what was here now.

As I grew up, the wishing didn't stop. It only shifted to a new goalpost: *I will be happy … when I lose the extra pounds, when the kids are out of diapers, when the student loans are paid, when I can go on vacation.*

And yet, when those wished-for future moments finally came to be, I couldn't help thinking how things should have been better, could have been different. And an internal judgmental voice asked, "Why did you say that? How could you have done that?"

I was showered with thoughts of *shoulda, woulda, coulda.* I was my own worst judge, critical of everything I thought and did. The internal judge gave no mercy for effort, circumstances, or lack of knowledge. The judge ruled by the standard of perfection—perfection of situations and actions, perfection of dialogue and responses, things in and out of my control.

The judgement of perfection was administered cruelly, constantly, and personally. This judging voice played a tape of past imperfections over and over in my head, reminding me of transgressions of the past and telling me that they were not forgiven. This judge would even dredge up incidents of regret specifically when things seemed to be going well. "Yeah, but remember the time you said *that*?!"

I would never say the things that the judge repeated to me to any other being. I would never have stayed in the presence of another human if they had talked to me the way the judge in my head did. I was in a relationship that was abusive—with myself.

The abuse went on for years. Meanwhile, I very convincingly presented that I was confident, strong and an overachiever. I hid my internal battle well.

Happiness was so fleeting for me. It was always the carrot on the stick. *Just keep going, you will eventually get it*, I would tell myself. There was one key. It came into my life when I was in a desperate place. I had gained forty pounds after my second pregnancy. I remember asking my husband if I was getting too fat for him. He didn't say no.

I started reading books about losing weight. What I found was a daily gratitude practice that was so simple I didn't quite believe it could really make a difference. But when gratitude arrived, I felt like happiness did as well.

I started small. Each night, I would write five things about which I could be grateful. Some days the pickings of gratitude were tiny mustard seeds. *Running water, flush toilets, a bed to sleep in, not yelling at the kids, a pen to write with*. As I continued, I saw the bits and pieces of the day in a new light. A peek of sunshine on an overcast day was a moment to pause for gratitude. Safe travel. Money to buy groceries. A warm shower. All things previously lumped into the day for the sake of just getting by.

Two psychologists, Dr. Robert A. Emmons of the University of California, Davis, and Dr. Michael E. McCullough of the University of Miami, have done groundbreaking research on gratitude. In one study, they asked three groups of people to write a few sentences each week about things that had happened to them during that time. The first group wrote about things they were grateful for. The second, about things that had made them irritated or unhappy. The last group stayed neutral, writing about both positive and negative events. Emmons and McCullough discovered that people whose writing focused on gratitude were more optimistic and happier. They even felt better physically, exercising more and visited their doctors less often.

I used gratitude as a comeback to the internal judge, as a way to tell the judge in my head to SHUT UP! I chose to listen to a kind, mentoring voice that wanted to help me grow through acceptance. Sure, things are not always the way I would prefer, but I am grateful for what is.

I practiced accepting kindness. I wasn't very good at believing kind and compassionate thoughts about myself. It was a practice, and practice means work. The judge put up a fight and regularly shared disapproval, to which I practiced saying that I no longer respected the thoughts of the judge, who would be silenced furthermore.

Through practice, perseverance, and persistence, the kind, loving mentor is the guiding voice helping me to be in gratitude for what is.

REFLECTION

Gratitude is a popular word and sentiment. But it need not be cliché, because gratitude, when felt, is never wasted. How can you add more moments of gratitude to your life? How can you purposefully fold a practice of gratitude into your day?

The development of a gratitude practice can start with a piece of paper and a pen. You can use a journal and crayons. Your choice of paper and writing utensil is not what makes this practice magical. Some days you might have to dig deep, really reach for it, but it is there. Pick three things and write them down. The things you choose to write down may be general and large, like fair weather or ocean life, or it might be something very specific, like a cup of coffee in your favorite mug or a hug from a friend. The feelings generated and the gratitude felt by starting with three things on a simple piece of paper can roll over into your everyday life. Instead of reflecting back at the end of your day searching for moments to be grateful about, the day will be filled with moments that you recognize in real time, adding to the magical power of your practice.

Crying for Days

❧

"The winds of grace blow all the time.
All we need to do is set our sails."

—RAMAKRISHNA

When I was twenty-two, I didn't know how to separate the thoughts in my head from the feelings and emotions that overwhelmed me. Crying one moment and laughing the next. Laughing one moment and angry the next. Angry one moment and afraid the next. Emotions can bring us to the depths of despair, to the mountains of ecstasy, and to all the places inbetween. After I gave birth to my first baby I was overwhelmed with thoughts that I had no idea what I was doing and that it would be a miracle if this child survived. The thoughts came so easily, I knew they must be true.

Gabrielle was the name we gave our precious bundle. She came into this world with her own strong personality and a voice that wanted to be shared. This tiny baby had perseverance. Crying for what seemed like no reason was intermixed with the crying for being hungry, tired, or wanting a dry diaper. The daytime crying was sporadic, but the main event would start at 5 p.m. almost on the dot and would last until at least 10 p.m. This was not an off-and-on fussiness. This was full-on, constant crying. As a new mother, I was alarmed and worried that something was wrong. When I asked our doctor and other mothers—some who had babies who also cried in abundance—I was given a lot of advice. Hubby and I tried our best. We rocked, we walked, we bounced, we bundled tightly, we bundled loosely, we laid down, we sat up. Maybe it was me. I ate differently, I ate less, I ate more, and yet still she cried and cried some more. Those evening crying bouts were unnerving as one week became two, then three. The doctor said she would grow out of it. But then: More days, more crying.

I felt horrible that I was not able to comfort my child. I was desperate for her to stop crying, which would stop the pain I felt in my heart, stop the feeling that I was not a good enough mother, stop the feeling of guilt that I could not handle the crying with grace and ease. On one particular day, Gabrielle had been crying constantly for hours and it was still only early afternoon. I was exhausted and overwhelmed by my lack of mothering skills. I knew that this crying episode was just the preview to the evening's rerun. Holding her in front of me, I shouted at the top of my lungs, "I DON'T KNOW WHAT TO DO!"

This startled her, and the crying turned to wailing. I joined her in the wailing. Frustration continued to arise in my body, and in a sharp instant I realized I needed to put this baby down—immediately! I laid her in her crib, both of us still wailing, and I quickly exited the bedroom and slammed the door. I walked across the hall into our bedroom and collapsed onto the bed. I trembled with the realization of how easily my frustration could have gotten out of control. I had just wanted her understand that I just wanted her to be okay, and that I needed her to stop crying. The impulse to shake my dear baby, to try to make her understand, was an extension of my frustration and my anger at myself for not being able to make her feel better.

Gradually, I calmed down, my tears spent. My heart filled with empathy for people who did not have a stop mechanism on their frustration, and so might shake a baby to get them to stop crying. I knew the ramifications of shaking a baby: brain damage or death. I knew I would never allow myself to do something so dangerous. I also knew the feeling of frustration that I could not communicate to a tiny baby my desire for her to be comfortable, which would in turn bring me comfort as well.

As I lay on the bed feeling defeated, my feelings shifted to my fear that I was an incompetent mother, knowing how easily my frustration could have led to a terrible conclusion. But by the grace of God, this power outside of myself prompted me to lay Gabrielle down, shut the door, and give myself breathing room. I was doing my best. That was all I could do. As I learned more, I would do better, and we would make it through to another day.

REFLECTION

We don't expect a newborn child to come into this world with the ability to talk and walk and take care of business. We know that when everything is new, time is needed for learning. Yet, when it comes to our adult selves, we seem to forget this. We fail to give ourselves mercy for not knowing or needing time to learn.

But mercy is not just for newborns and other people. Mercy is also for ourselves. In fact, the person in your life most deserving of mercy is *you*. Don't skip this reflection if you don't believe me. Just because you don't believe me doesn't make it true.

We can be harder on ourselves than anyone else. We allow berating, negative thoughts to go on incessantly. But what would happen if you took a pause from the words of condemnation and just told yourself that it was okay. *You* are okay.

Imagine yourself as a little child of two or three years old. What would you say to your child self? What tenderness would you show? What soothing sounds would you use? How would you embrace this wee one with love?

This practice of connecting with the core of who you are is where the gift of self-love and self-compassion meet. Give yourself the kindness you deserve.

Post Office

❦

"Life shrinks or expands according to one's courage."

—ANAIS NIN

An auction in a small town is a time of gathering for the locals, giving everyone an opportunity to visit and catch up on what is new. A neighbor down the street was moving to an apartment across town, and held an auction for her unwanted belongings. The street was blocked at the corners with auction signs and orange cones—not that anyone could drive through, because there were hayracks parked in the middle of the street filled with the contents of once-overstuffed closets and corners. Furniture was placed in rows on the front lawn. Chairs sat side by side next to the vacuum, next to the spare bed, next to the dehumidifier. How long an auction lasts is largely determined by the number of hayracks filled with treasures. This neighbor was a substantial saver during her lifetime, so there were four full racks.

I ran into Mike at the auction. I had known him for many years, because he lived in town and we used to be coworkers. We exchanged pleasantries and he asked what was new. I shared that I had started my own massage therapy business, and was working out of an office in my home. Mike hadn't been aware of this yet. Our conversation continued for a bit longer, then we made our way closer to the auction racks to make sure we didn't miss the bid on the items we were eyeing.

Finding out that someone I knew in town hadn't heard that I had opened a business surprised me. This was a wakeup call to more actively market my new endeavor. I had been telling family and friends, past clients and colleagues, but I needed to get the word out. I needed to let others know that I was actively taking new clients, so when someone needed a massage, they would think of Tanya's Healing Hands and call me.

My first steps were to print up some flyers and go to local businesses on Main Street and hang them up on their bulletin boards. Initially, I thought of four businesses I was comfortable approaching because I knew the owners and they already knew I was in business. I had a business coach at the time who suggested I approach *all* the businesses. It sounds so simple, doesn't it? For some people jumping out into the light of "look at me" is easy and natural. For me, it was a process of waffling between *oh my goodness someone will think I am a crazy lady* and *you won't have a business if you don't.* Marketing Tanya's Healing Hands seemed mostly doable, but for some reason I had an amazing amount of fear around putting up a flyer in the post office. Everyone in town had to go to the post office to get their mail. In this gathering place, townsfolk would see the declaration that I was open for business.

I was afraid of being called a crazy lady. Honestly, in some people's minds, I *was* a bit crazy. I had quit a job I had been in for over eight years—a steady, well-paying job where I had been working with great people. I quit that job to go to massage therapy school. This was at a time when massage therapy was new to the area and still looked at as a luxury, not an option for taking care of your body, mind and spirit. My daughters were in kindergarten and second grade back then, and I woke those little girls up before the sun came up to bring them to daycare so that I could commute three and a half hours each day to attend massage therapy school for eleven months.

With flyers in hand, I made my first stop, the post office. I pulled my car into a parking spot and shut the engine off. I took a deep breath and reached for a poster and thumbtacks. After another deep breath, I pushed myself out of the car, walked into the lobby, and saw there was no one there. I pinned up the poster, opened my own mailbox to retrieve the mail, and walked out. No one shouted at me that I was crazy. No one told me to take the sign down because I didn't deserve to be in business. No one even noticed that I was walking through the fire of my own resistance and putting my heart on the bulletin board. If "they" were going to let me go along my business of sharing my gifts with the world, then who was I to stop?

REFLECTION

When I sat in the car readying myself to expand into a space of being seen, I paused to take some breaths. Here is a breathing practice to help you breathe a little deeper, a little slower, and calm the sympathetic nervous system. This is a practice that can be done any time to help you relax or get grounded.

Start by taking a few natural breaths. Feel the breath move in and out of your body. After a few breaths, while you inhale, count to three. Pause at the top of the breath for the count of one and then exhale fully to the count of three and then pause again for the count of one. Breathe a few times, counting to three on each inhalation and exhalation. Continue to breathe in to the count of three and now make the exhale longer, perhaps 4, 5 or 6 counts. Continue this for a few more rounds or until you feel the breathing practice is complete. Return your breath to its natural rhythm. Notice any changes in the ease of your breath. Watch for more relaxation throughout the body.

Bats

༝

*"The baby bat
Screamed out in fright,
'Turn on the dark,
I'm afraid of the light."*

—SHEL SILVERSTEIN

I have always been afraid of bats. Luckily, for the rest of my family, curiosity proved stronger than fear.

My first close encounter with a bat was when I was an adult, the year Gabby was two. We were living in a rental house, and hubby was trying to get a few hours' sleep before working the night shift. I was sitting in our brown recliner in the living room reading a book in the moments of quiet before I went to bed. I looked up from my book when some movement caught my eye. Something was moving near the top of the curtains. With a growing sense of dread, I looked again more closely. It was a bat! My screaming ensued. Hubby finally came out of the bedroom, sleepy and dazed. I told him I'd seen a bat. Instead of jumping into action, he turned around to go back to the bedroom.

"What the hell are you doing?" I shouted. "There is a bat in the house! Protect me!"

I was shocked that there was no urgency in his movements, no hurry to get this vile creature out of my house. He came back out of the bedroom and asked if we had a box.

"A box? How are you going to kill it with a box?" I said.

"Bats are endangered and illegal to kill," he explained.

"What? Are you kidding me?"

We found a box in the basement, along with a flat piece of cardboard, and brought them upstairs for this rescue mission. Hubby pressed the open side of the box against the curtain, and asked me to hand him the cardboard. I was not excited to get any closer to the bat than I already was—on the opposite side of the room. But I walked over and handed him the cardboard. As he slid the flat piece behind the box, the bat lost its grip on the curtain and fell into the box. We both jumped at the sound of it moving inside.

"Open the door," he said.

I gladly opened the door to give him space to rid my house of the bat. Hubby stood in the doorway and threw everything—bat, box, and cardboard—into the front yard.

When he closed the door, I was puzzled. "That's it? You're just going to leave it in the yard?"

"You can go pick up the box if you want," Hubby said.

I declined, knowing I would feel safer in the morning light.

We went to inspect the attic. Hubby pointed out all the piles that looked like dirt. I'm sorry to say they were not. Those piles were bat poop. *Oh, hell no!* I called our landlord and told him we needed an exterminator. In the meantime, I anxiously and religiously checked all the curtains.

One night a while later, before the exterminator visited, I was in bed reading a Stephen King novel while hubby was working the night shift. I heard a sound coming from the attic.

The noise moved swiftly from the west side to the east and back again. I could hear scratching noises, a sound like tiny feet running back and forth, and even some screeching, although that was from my own throat. I put my head under the covers and called my husband at work.

"Aliens are playing soccer in our attic!" I exclaimed.

Convincing as this sounded to me at the time, in my defense my bedtime reading had given me a heightened awareness of the supernatural. Hubby was less convinced. "I hardly think there are aliens playing soccer in our attic," he said. I took the phone from under the covers and reached toward the ceiling to let him hear the skittering noise, which continued to move from one side of the ceiling to the other. The sound didn't travel well over the phone lines. Having him tell me it was likely the bats leaving or coming into the attic *did not* comfort me. Luckily, the exterminator eventually came and the bats went away.

My next interaction with a bat happened when the girls were about five and seven. It was a lovely summer evening. I was getting supper ready and the girls and Hubby were all outside in the backyard. I went out into the garage to put some cans into the recycling. I heard a noise inside the bin, and lifted the lid to investigate. Inside, I saw a bat climbing around among the bottles and paper. I stepped back and stifled a gasp. Acting cool and moderately collected, I went into the back yard and told hubby to please come and take care of the unwanted visitor. I must have still had some trembling in my voice, because the girls caught on that something was happening and became very excited. As I looked on from behind the safety of the front window, hubby picked up the bat in his gloved hands, walked with it to the front yard, and placed it in a tree,. Bats cannot just flap their wings and lift off the ground, like birds. They must drop and then they are able to fly.

We had a lively family discussion about bats that night around the supper table, retelling the story of the bat on the curtain and a few stories from hubby's childhood. Ariel, who was five, wanted to go outside and look for the mommy bat. She was sure that the one we found was a baby because it was so small. When I told her that the bat in the garage was likely a mommy bat, she looked at me incredulously.

"If that is all the bigger they get, why would you be scared of them?" Ah, the insights of children.

Our last family bat encounter happened at Disney's Animal Kingdom. I'm sure you can imagine how I felt as we walked into the bat exhibit. As we approached the enclosure on the far side of the room, my family kept looking at me with wry smiles, because they all knew that bats were not my favorite animal. I huddled close to my family as they observed the little flying beasts. Some were as big as two feet long, hanging from a tree behind the glass. I kept breathing as deeply as possible, not wanting to let my disdain show. One of my daughters, with urging from her father, reached forward. I was surprised by what happened when her hand reached the glass—or, I should say, where where I expected the glass to be. It took me an extra beat to realize that these bats were not behind glass. It was an aviary, an open habitat for the bats. There was no glass in this exhibit at all! I beelined it right into the hallway, while my family laughed heartily.

My family still teases me, with love, about my bat encounters. I laugh with everyone else, glad that my family could teach me about the care and appreciation of bats and happy that I have moved past my fear of these creatures into merely a mild repulsion.

REFLECTION

We all have fears. And fear has the power to stop us. But curiosity motivates us. Here is a practice in exploring curiosity. A fear statement might sound like, "I can't ask for a raise at work. They will just say no!" The challenge is to make curiosity stronger than fear. Start with a an "I wonder" statement. "*I wonder* what will happen when I ask for a raise at work?"

"I wonder" statements are full of curiosity. These statements set aside our tendency to prejudge what you *think* will happen, and allow for the exploration of what might be.

Try it. When you feel yourself going to a place of fear, instead of stopping, shift the fearful thought into one of curiosity— "I wonder..."—and see where it might take you.

Ruts

❧

"What are heavy? Sea-sand and sorrow;
What are brief? Today and tomorrow;
What are frail? Spring blossoms and youth."

—CHRISTINA ROSETTI

It was a lovely spring day, the sun shining and warming the skin in a way not felt since the previous fall. I was home from my freshman year in college and I wanted to go visit my grandparents. They lived a half-mile away as the crow flies, and two miles by road. I always took the road. Except for today. My eighth-grade brother was home from school, and I asked him if he wanted to drive across the field in the old blue Chevy '68 pickup and go visit Grandma and Grandpa. He really wanted to go, or maybe he just didn't want to do his homework. Either way, he said yes.

This old pickup had been our farm truck for as long as I remember. It was used for errands, running back and forth to fields, picking up parts or bringing lunch out to the field. The first time I drove it, I was thirteen. My dad needed to measure a field, and he wanted me to drive the pickup on the road to the other side of the field. I wasn't sure I could handle it—it was a straight-stick manual transmission. Dad assured me that I just had to leave it in first gear, drive down the road, and wait for him on the corner. I drove so slowly that my dad practically beat me to the corner. In that mile of road, I drove two miles weaving back and forth from one side to the other.

Taking the trusty ol' blue pickup, Eric and I drove off the yard through a small section of pasture into the black fertile soil of the field yet to be planted. We didn't get far before the tires started to sink—and so did my stomach. I had forgotten that when the frost comes out of the ground, the fields are a sloppy mess of mud. Revving the engine did not help the tires escape the muddy suction. We were stuck with the tires buried halfway in mud. If we got out of here, there were going to be some significant ruts in this field.

As a farm girl, I knew ruts were a bad deal. Ruts in a field cause problems like uneven land for driving a tractor and planter, making seeding uneven. Compaction of the soil can also be an issue: It makes it more difficult for the water and nutrients to move through the soil.

I panicked. What was my father going to say? How much damage had my dim-witted plan done? How much extra work had I just caused for my father? But first, how were we going to get this pickup out of the field?

My little brother saved the day. It was his idea to put a couple of boards under the back tires to get enough traction to spin us free. Mud flew high as I gunned it, trying to move quickly away from my bad idea. Mud flew off the tires and into the air as we made it onto the gravel road and turned the corner to get to Grandma and Grandpa's.

At supper that night, I told my dad that I'd had a little adventure. I apologized for the ruts and careless decision of trying to go across the field in the spring. My father didn't say anything. He just continued to eat his supper. My heart raced a bit, expecting a harsh word. But he didn't criticize or holler or anything.

I tried to understand his silence. Maybe he thought there was no reason to say anything, because nothing could be said to change the situation. Maybe he thought I was past the need of a lecture because of my age. Maybe he was just tired and this was not what he wanted to put any energy toward.

I was aware of the difference in how my dad treated me and how he would have treated my brother. I had a realization: I was my father's favorite. Or, at least, I was treated much differently than my brother. I knew that if my brother had done what I did, there would have been a verbal lambasting. And yet, here I was sitting in silence. The weight of what was not said was heavier than any punishment.

REFLECTION

There is an ancient Hawaiian healing practice called Hoʻoponopono.

It has four steps that seem as though they would be too simple to have any effect, and yet, again and again, people have found healing.

Whenever a place for healing presents itself in your life, open to the place where the hurt resides within you. After identifying this place, with as much feeling as you can, say the four statements below:

- *I love you.*
- *I'm sorry.*
- *Please forgive me.*
- *Thank you.*

This is the complete practice. It is done for yourself and within yourself. The phrases can be repeated over and over, mean what you say, feel it. This is a practice of love. And there is nothing more powerful than love.

Crossings

❧

*"Let go of the idea that the path will lead to your goal.
The truth is that with each step we take, we arrive."*

—PAULO COELHO, THE WITCH OF PORTOBELLO

When I was in kindergarten, after the school day was finished, I would wait for the big kids—second-graders!—and we would cross the street and walk to Dottie's daycare. Then I would have a snack and play until my mother would pick me up.

"I'll be picking you up from school today," my mom told me one morning. When the school day ended, I stood outside and waited. Other children left with their parents, walked to the buses and crossed the street with the help of the crossing guard. The big kids who went to Dottie's crossed the street and started on their way, too. When I didn't join them, the crossing guard asked me if I needed to cross the street, too. I was at an internal crossroads. My mother had told me that she would pick me up, but she wasn't there, and another adult questioned my belief that I knew what to do. I made the only decision that made sense to me: I crossed the street with the crossing guard and started walking in the only direction that I knew to go. I walked to Dottie's.

When I arrived at Dottie's, my mother was there as well.

"Why did you leave school?" she asked. "I told you I was going to pick you up, and now we are late." But at five years old, I didn't have the ability to think through all the options and outcomes. I stood and waited at the crosswalk, and even though I knew my mother said she was going to pick me up, she wasn't there. At that moment I made a choice. From the age of five well into adulthood, I judged myself when making choices, and felt I couldn't trust myself.

I internalized my mother's words and tone of voice to mean that I had made a wrong choice. A wrong choice that caused her to be upset. As I continued throughout my life, there were many times when I struggled to make decisions because I didn't want to make a wrong choice. And I didn't want someone else to be upset with me because of a choice I had made. I analyzed my options, and stewed over what choice was right.

As I sat at the kitchen counter talking about options, my mom would tell me to do whatever my little heart desired. She meant this to mean that I should feel free to dream and follow my dreams, but her statement didn't feel real. I still had this belief that it was important not to make a wrong choice.

I now realize that each choice does not have to be right or wrong. Each choice is just that: a choice, but not the *only* choice. Options have potential. If the outcome is not what we desired, we can make another choice—sometimes it is a choice of circumstance, and other times a choice in attitude. We have the ability to make a choice all the time. The potential is limitless.

REFLECTIONS

Choices can feel easy and fun, or paralyzing and dangerous. We can free-flow with options, or feel constricted and freeze.

When you are feeling stuck and not able to make a decision, it can be helpful to press pause. Let the decision be and do something else. A great option is to *dance*! Yes, that's right, dance. Find your favorite dance tune, turn it up to eleven, and move!

After a few minutes of dancing, check in with your body. How are you feeling? Perhaps the decision you needed to make will have a clearer answer, even if it doesn't you will have moved your body, shaken up the stagnation of mental energy, and taken in a few full breaths.

Heart Opening

❧

"I tell you this
to break your heart,
by which I mean only
that it break open and never close again
to the rest of the world."

—MARY OLIVER, "LEAD," NEW AND SELECTED POEMS, VOL. 2

No one and nothing could have prepared me for what being pregnant and giving birth would do to my heart. I believed I could feed a baby, change its diapers, and hold it as it slept, but could I really love a child?

After she arrived, there were lots of times we were both crying. We were both in the same boat, neither of us having a clue. Even though I felt lost, floating by myself in the sea of motherhood, I loved my little baby girl with such fierceness I shocked even myself. When hubby and I decided to try for a second baby, I was fearful that this maternal heart love would have no space for baby number two. I loved my firstborn so much that I seriously doubted I could love another in the same way. My mind went on rampages imagining the awful life this second child would have, knowing that her mother's heart was only capable of loving one child. I knew logically that other people had multiple children and they were loved well. But fear is not a logical beast.

I even asked my doctor, whom I highly respected: "What is wrong with me?"

He assured me it would be fine. In my mind, I left my snarky response unspoken: *What did he really know?* He was the parent of only one child and, besides, he wasn't a mother. Surely he was misguided in thinking he knew anything about my dysfunctional heart and mothering capabilities.

As it turns out, my heart did not need to break in two. My love did not need to split and splinter in order to share my love between my two children. Instead it grew exponentially. My love exploded to include both my children fully.

As my children grew, they would sometimes complain that my love for them was unevenly divided. It never has been. There were days I told them I didn't like what they did or how they acted, but I always loved them.

From before birth to adulthood, my children have been teachers for me. At times my heart has skipped beats, been bruised and even broken by those teachers. They have also helped my heart to heal, gather strength, and to open to love another human without expectations and barriers.

REFLECTION

Love, this emotion and feeling that is both noun and verb, can mean differrent things depending on what you say. *I love chocolate. I love Grandma. I love rugby.* All these statements express love, but in varying degrees. It is a straitjacket of the English language. Thankfully, our hearts, while connected with language, can expressively connect with love on a vibrational level. Use the following practice to expand and feel the vibrations of love that are within you.

Come to a comfortable space. Your eyes may be open or closed. Allow your breath to be relaxed and natural. Imagine brilliant white light in your heart center. This white light is pure love. Allow this white light to expand and move throughout your body. Allow it to encompass and move into all of your organs, your tissues, cells and all the spaces around the cells. The brilliant white light of love moves down your arms and legs. Allow the light to move out your fingertips and out the bottom of your feet. Continue breathing comfortably. And when you feel complete, place your hands on your heart and take a deep breath.

Laundry

૨૪

"The cloud is free only to go with the wind.
The rain is free only in falling."

—WENDELL BERRY

My first memory of laundry is the crisp, sweet smell of sheets as I ran through them while they hung on the line.

My mother and grandmother told me I was such a big help because I was keeping the flies off the sheets while they dried. There were two metal poles twenty feet apart with a cylinder of cement in the ground to secure them. Thick gauged wire was wound between one pole and the other three times, and at one side hung a bucket of wooden clothespins. I would run through the sheets until I reached the pole, and then I would boomerang myself back to the opposite side, giggling and smiling, making up songs and stories, back and forth and back and forth, sometimes until well after the sheets were dried. I still love the smell of sheets dried in the sunshine and fresh air.

As I grew, I helped with laundry too, but never with the sorting and washing, only with hanging wet clothes on the line in the summer. The first time I needed to do laundry at college, I was terrified. The cycles, spins, and knobs were a mystery to me. I figured out the basics and decided this was a job best done at long intervals. I even bought extra pairs of underwear for the sole purpose of extending the time between trips to the basement, five flights down.

Laundry for my own family changed the first time someone asked me why the shirt they wanted to wear was not clean. This momma stopped, raised her eyebrows, and said, "I have a solution for *that*!" My family was taught how the buttons on the washer worked real quick. This was not a huge leap, since they already helped sort and fold and sometimes even put away the laundry. I didn't worry that when they left home they wouldn't know how to use a washer or dryer.

In 2002 I took a mission trip to San Lucas Toliman Mission in Guatemala. One day was spent working with mission staff in a village that had sustained catastrophic damage from mudslides after a hurricane. Help from NGOs, the government, and the mission supported the villagers in relocating the entire village and building homes. Families lived in transitional shacks until permanent homes could be built. Our job was to move the transitional frames to new locations to make room for permanent homes.

After one afternoon of work, a woman asked us if we would move her wash basin from the transitional space to her permanent home. This wasn't easy. The basin was made of concrete and weighed over 800 pounds. It struck me that this utilitarian piece of equipment was a brightly colored turquoise. Throughout my time in Guatemala, I saw basins colored turquoise, yellow, pink, blue, and green—a stark difference to the muted and basic colors traditionally seen in the states.

As a group, we assessed the situation and organized a plan for the transfer. There were six of us on the job. We lifted, moved, rested, asked why we thought we could do this, and then kept on until the basin was at its new home. The woman showered us with praise and gratitude. I could see that having this "pila," as it is called in Guatemala, close to her house was going to make her daily life easier. The pila is used for washing both laundry and dishes. She would still need to haul water from the local water supply until the water pipes serving her home were connected.

The hard work of moving the basin paled in comparison to having to haul water and hand-wash laundry.

On the following day as I took a walk by the lake, I watched women stand knee-deep in the water and scrub their clothes on rocks, then place them to dry on rocks and bushes on shore. My gratitude for running water and washing machines expanded.

All of these laundry experiences give me pause. I choose never to complain about laundry. I do not have to haul my family's clothes to a lake, stand in the water, and scrub them upon a rock. I don't have to haul water to a basin outside of my house either. For me, doing laundry is a time to deliberately shift into a space of gratitude. A task that can be a symbol of love for family, a teaching of independence, or even a breath of fresh air.

REFLECTION

Gratitude is not only a feeling but can also manifest as action. Marie Kondo, the Japanese super-organizer and founder of the KonMari Method of tidying up, suggests that with regard to discarding clutter or organizing, if you find something that no longer brings you joy, you thank the item and release it.

This week find a few things in your space that no longer bring you joy and, with gratitude, release them. Removing clutter does not have to be a large project of drudgery. It can be as simple as finding something that no longer brings you joy that can be removed from your space and in turn bless someone else. Make it fun. Just release the things that don't bring you joy and keep the things that do.

Vegas

❧

"Some changes happen deep down inside of you. And the truth is, only you know about them. Maybe that's the way it's supposed to be."

—JUDY BLUME, TIGER EYES

As I drifted off to sleep that Friday night in Vegas, a voice not my own meandered through my head, asking "What if a man tells you that you're attractive?"

"Whatever!?" my own voice in my head said.

The voice replied, "'That is the lesson."

And then I fell asleep.

I was on a girl's trip. A group of friends that took a yearly trip for a long weekend somewhere different to relax, laugh, and hangout in each other's company. Saturday was a wonderfully hot and sunny day in Las Vegas. We spent the day at the pool, we drank adult beverages, cooled off in the water, made each other laugh, took naps in the sunshine, and visited with others at the pool. In the evening, we ventured out to eat, walk the Strip, people watch, take in a few sights of Vegas at night, and dance.

We were all laughing and enjoying the freedom of being ourselves with friends when a few gentlemen joined us on the dance floor. We'd chatted with these gentlemen earlier at the pool—but it's quite hard to have a conversation on a dance floor with music playing enthusiastically loud. Our snippets of conversations consisted of leaning an ear in close to hear and speaking closely when responding. We moved from a dancing circle to pairs of dancers, still talking with closeness needed for conversation. The man I was dancing with leaned in and said to me, "You are so beautiful, I wish I could kiss you right now."

Infidelity, no matter how easily accessible, was not a souvenir I was going to bring home from Vegas. My mind jumped back to that moment the night before, when I had been falling asleep, and the voice said, "What if a man tells you, you are attractive?"

I shook my head and rolled my eyes. I said to the man, "Whatever."

This man had told me he was a negotiator for his profession. "You must be good at your job, because you are full of it!" I laughed. He didn't. "We're in Vegas. I am guessing because this is a yearly business trip for you, you are used to some of the perks of the motto 'what happens in Vegas, stays in Vegas.'"

He squinted in offense, as if he took my scoffing of his compliment personally. This took me aback. I had never paid attention to the way men responded to my rebuttals. I was so caught up in the rightness of my thoughts and feelings that I was not pretty or beautiful, but that I was fat and unattractive. I never once considered that if someone gave me a compliment, they were actually sharing their truth.

My arsenal of ways to deflect compliments is well-stocked. Up to this point I had never, ever, taken a compliment about my looks from a man. I always, *always*, assumed it was a lie. I had never even taken a compliment from my husband.

But in this moment, I saw a layer of truth that I had denied. I was well-practiced in the art of letting others own their truth around life, actions, and personal beliefs ... except, it would seem, when it came to me. I felt an imbalance of truth. I realized that I was not allowed to use my truth as a paintbrush, to whitewash over the top of anyone else's truth even when their truth was about me.

After returning from Vegas, I pondered the whole experience. I had a flash of a memory. I was fifteen, in the car with my mom, and she told me a story of her own youth. At the end of the story, she said, "Boys are only nice and give compliments because they want something from you." *Bam!* This sentence had stuck in my unconscious and altered every interaction I had with the opposite sex. I unknowingly held on to this belief for over twenty-five years.

This was the lesson. I did not have to hold this belief any longer. I could release it. The next time my husband gave me a compliment, I didn't deflect it. I stood in the space of looking at what was true for him and I said, "Thank you honey, I love you." Lesson learned.

REFLECTION

Everyone has their own truths and points of view. Everyone experiences life through their own story lens. We are all the main character in our own movie. Everyone else plays a supporting role. And we play a supporting role in other people's movies, that is, lives, too. It is no wonder that our points of view are different even when many aspects of our lives are similar.

Imagine a burning building. You are one of three other people reporting for the local paper. Each of you is stationed at a different corner of the building. You can imagine that every story reported will differ, even though the event was identical. Life is the same way. Our perspective colors our story. Knowing this, we can shift into inquiry, using the question, "Isn't it interesting that I have this point of view?" I encourage you to look where you come into judgement about something. Take some time to write about your point of view and look at your point of view as interesting. Keep in mind that all points of view, yours and everyone's, are formed by their lens of life.

Conversation

❦

"In the end only three things matter: How much you loved, how gently you lived and how gracefully you let go of things not meant for you."

—ATTRIBUTED TO BUDDHA

What password had I seen her using earlier? Technology grew as my girls grew. iPods, flip phones, texting, Facebook, smartphones. As parents, we learned how to navigate these leaps as best we could around their needs and wants, and, of course, their wants cloaked as needs. One of our rules was that phones stayed in the kitchen when you went to bed.

I felt that as a mother of teenagers I had the right and duty to use info on their phones to help me make the best parental choices I could. I was a little sneaky, not because I wanted to catch them doing something wrong, but I wanted to see the truth unfiltered. When I used the password and opened her texts, a recent series of messages between her and her boyfriend revealed the fact that they were sexually active. I had an internal maternal freakout as a cornucopia of thoughts and emotions flooded through me. My baby girl was no longer a little girl, she was eighteen. She was able to make her own decisions. What was I going to do with this information?

When I grew up, my "sex talk" with my mom amounted to her pausing by my bedroom door as she tossed a Dear Abby pamphlet—or maybe it was Ann Landers—about sex and teenagers on my bed. "If you have any questions, you can ask me," she said. And with that she walked down the hall.

I decided to have a more open conversation with my girls. We talked about sex, abstinence, protected sex, emotions, feelings, consequences. But at this moment, the emotion of knowing my child was participating in this particular adult act was unsettling.

Sleep came in fits that night, but, still, I felt calmer in the morning. My husband and I decided that we needed to talk to both our daughter and her boyfriend. We felt it was important to talk about the emotional and physical ramifications of being sexually active.

Sunday evening came, and Dakota and Gabby were downstairs watching TV. I was in my office, not doing anything specific, just biding my time. Hubby came into the office and said, "Well, we should probably go talk with the kids."

But I could not stand up. I was glued to the chair. Every time I rose, I instantly sat back down. "I can't," I said. Then, "Okay, okay, okay." Then, "I can't." The up-and-down movements of my body matched my resolve as it came and went. This conversation felt impossible.

"Okay." I finally stood up and took a step towards the office door before sitting down again. "I need to breathe."

"Are you comfortable with this?" I asked Hubby as he calmly let me have my moments of crazy.

"I think it is important, so we need to do it, even if I am uncomfortable." Such wise words from my dear husband.

"Okay." I stood up and my stomach dropped again, but this time I stayed standing. Hubby had his arm around my shoulders and gave me a gentle squeeze of encouragement as we walked out of the office, down the hall, and to the top of the steps that led to the basement family room.

"Gabby, can you and Dakota come up here please." Up the stairs they came, not knowing why they were summoned. They had quizzical looks on their faces. Those shifted into looks of apprehension when I said, "Gabby, you come talk with me in the living room. Dakota and Dad are going to go outside to talk."

I was still a mess of nerves. Anxiousness spanning generations. Generations of shame around sex. Gabby looked at me expectantly, clearly thinking *"what's going on?"*, nervous with a twinge of cool teenage nonchalance. I sat on the sofa. Gabby chose the living room chair, which was angled towards the sofa to make conversation easier. She chose to sit in the chair with her legs over the arm on the side away from the couch.

I took a breath, trying not to let my emotion rise up into tears before even starting the conversation. I took another breath and paused. "Gabby, this is the hardest conversation that I have ever had to start." A deep breath, and I jumped into the conversation. "I know that you are having sex."

A look of denial passed her face, then she looked away and gazed out the window as if she was willing herself to be transported to anywhere else.

"No, we're…" she started.

"Stop. Don't deny it, I read your phone."

Tears formed in her eyes, and then in mine.

"It is important to your dad and me that you are safe and making decisions that support you and your health," I began. The conversation then wove through the practical options of safe sex, the emotional connections that happen, and our desire that she really knew that as her parents, we cared deeply, and that we were having this conversation out of love and acceptance of who she was.

Growing pains are not just physical for children, they are emotional, as well— for both child and parent. I chose to have this conversation with my daughter not because it was easy or even necessary. I chose to have the conversation so that the lines of communication would be open and clear for us in the moment and in the future, and, hopefully, for generations to come. When we finished our conversation, we ended with a big hug. I affirmed that I loved her and always would. I like to think that we stood in a circle of women from our family tree, releasing shame, embracing clear communication, and affirming love.

My conversation with my daughter didn't have to be so hard. But it was blanketed in shame. Shame around sexuality handed down by generations of family and church. How can we move past shame? Brené Brown has spent years researching shame. In her work she shares that once we recognize shame, we can respond by making mindful and thoughtful decisions. If we can't recognize shame, it blindsides us, and we want to slink away and hide.

One of the keys to shame resilience, the ability to move past shame, is making connections and building your social support network. Today, connect with your network. Reach out, talk, share and feel the support in becoming more shame-resilient.

Final Words

❧

"It can be hard to understand why a life is long enough."

—James Malecek's eulogy

Grandpa had exploratory surgery. They opened him up and just as quickly closed him. It was the beginning of the end. His body couldn't fight the cancer and also heal from surgery. He was at home on the farm when I went to visit for Grandma's birthday. We sat on the swivel chairs around the kitchen table under the window overlooking the farm. There, we visited as we always had, except this time Grandpa wasn't filled with his regular laughter and jokes. He was quiet, pale, and weak. It took a lot of effort for him to sit and visit, even for the short time we were there. It was the last time I saw him on the farm.

A few weeks later, Grandpa was admitted to the hospital for hospice care. As the end drew near, we were called as a family to say our goodbyes. We took turns going into his room by ourselves. I stood in the hallway and waited my turn. I was twenty-five, pregnant with my second daughter, and felt like a scared little girl, unsure of what was next. When it was my turn, I entered the dimly lit room. The bed was on the far side of the room. I walked over to Grandpa. He looked at me and held my hand. He spoke, but I couldn't understand him. He repeated himself, but I still didn't understand his words. He was medicated to help with the pain and his words were quiet and mumbled. I bent over the bed, gave him a hug, told him that I loved him, and rushed out of the room in tears. I was overcome with grief. I had said goodbye, but I didn't understand what he said—and I knew it would be the last time I would see him alive.

This moment was one of the reasons I was drawn to work and volunteer with hospice. I wanted to be a quiet presence for others who were mourning a loss as they said goodbye and were left to carry on. I wanted to sit by the bedside of a person passing on, to peacefully hold space and radiate love and calm. Not only for them, but to rewrite the script of the last time I saw my grandfather alive.

My father spoke at my grandfather's funeral. He directed a section just to us grandchildren:

After today do not mourn Grandpa's passing, but rather celebrate his life in the way you live yours. Remember the lessons of life he taught you.

Remember him for his outlook on life and the future.

Remember him for his willingness to help when needed.

Remember him for his love of all you children.

And remember him for his sense of humor. I cannot help but think that you will all be better people because of knowing him.

I treasure all of the memories I have of my grandfather, his personality and the gifts of wisdom that came through his life. I think of him every time I sit in vigil at a hospice patient's bed. At those times, I think I hear Grandpa whispering in my ear, "I am proud of you and I love you."

REFLECTION

Having a special person in our lives leave through death brings up many emotions. We can reflect on the unfairness of the timing and the despair brought on by the loss. We can swim in the tides of sorrow. We can also find the moments of laughter of a well-lived life, no matter the length. We can find the tender places of love in the embrace of other loved ones, a whisper of a scent that brings them to remembrance.

Those special to us may be gone from this physical world—and where their next adventure took them we will not know. But their spirit and personality are linked with us through the ether, never too far away.

How can you honor the memories of those special to you? Try writing them a letter of gratitude. Share with them your feelings and memories. Then read the letter aloud, imagining that they are sitting in front of you hearing all you want to share. When this is complete, you can ceremoniously burn the letter, releasing all the gratitude it encompasses into the universe.

About the Author

❧

Tanya Hanson leads retreats in the US and Internationally, inspiring her clients to find joy, grace and ease in their lives with a healthy dose of fun. She uses skills gained throughout her life experiences as a massage therapist, energy practitioner, yoga instructor, volunteer, business owner and life long learner to open up the space of possibilities for those that attend her events.

She and her husband Chad, are enthusiastic grandparents, they live in northern Minnesota and have two grown daughters.

More information can be found at www.tanyahanson.co about Tanya's workshops, retreats and online offerings.

www.ingramcontent.com/pod-product-compliance
Lightning Source LLC
LaVergne TN
LVHW020424290425
809865LV00007B/171